CITY

Thomas
Cook

WHAT'S IN YOUR GUIDEBOOK?

Independent authors Impartial up-to-date information from our travel experts who meticulously source local knowledge.

Experience Thomas Cook's 165 years in the travel industry and guidebook publishing enriches every word with expertise you can trust.

Travel know-how Thomas Cook has thousands of staff working around the globe, all living and breathing travel.

Editors Travel-publishing professionals, pulling everything together to craft a perfect blend of words, pictures, maps and design.

You, the traveller We deliver a practical, no-nonsense approach to information, geared to how you really use it.

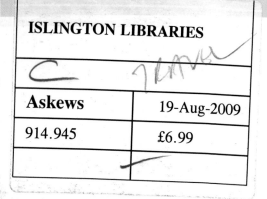

CITYSPOTS
ZURICH

Thomas
Cook

Written by Teresa Fisher
Updated by Marc Krebs

Published by Thomas Cook Publishing
A division of Thomas Cook Tour Operations Limited
Company registration No: 1450464 England
The Thomas Cook Business Park, 9 Coningsby Road
Peterborough PE3 8SB, United Kingdom
Email: books@thomascook.com, Tel: +44 (0)1733 416477
www.thomascookpublishing.com

Produced by The Content Works Ltd
Aston Court, Kingsmead Business Park, Frederick Place
High Wycombe, Bucks HP11 1LA
www.thecontentworks.com

Series design based on an original concept by Studio 183 Limited

ISBN: 978-1-84848-062-9

First edition © 2007 Thomas Cook Publishing
This second edition © 2009 Thomas Cook Publishing
Text © Thomas Cook Publishing
Maps © Thomas Cook Publishing/PCGraphics (UK) Limited
Transport map © Communicarta Limited

Series Editor: Lucy Armstrong
Production/DTP: Steven Collins

Printed and bound in Spain by GraphyCems

Cover photography (St-Peterskirche) © 1Apix/Alamy

CONTENTS

SYMBOLS KEY

The following symbols are used throughout this book:

ⓐ address ☏ telephone ⓦ website address ⓛ opening times
Ⓝ public transport connections ❶ important

The following symbols are used on the maps:

ℹ️ information office		▮	points of interest
✈ airport		O	city
➕ hospital		O	large town
🛡 police station		○	small town
🚌 bus station		=	motorway
➡ railway station		—	main road
✝ cathedral		—	minor road
❶ numbers denote featured		—	railway
cafés & restaurants			

Hotels and restaurants are graded by approximate price as follows:
£ budget price **££** mid-range price **£££** expensive

In addresses, 'Strasse' and '-strasse' (meaning 'street' or 'road')
are abbreviated to 'Str.' and '-str.'; 'Platz' and '-platz' (meaning
'square') are abbreviated to 'Pl.' and '-pl.'

◗ *The twin spires of Grossmünster*

Introduction

There's more to Switzerland's largest city than gold bars and chocolate bars. It's a classical city with a contemporary edge, preserving its architectural and cultural heritage yet surprising the world with the latest innovations in art and architecture, fashion, shopping and design.

● *The River Limmat cuts through the historic Altstadt*

Forget the old image of a characterless and cold-hearted financial city of buttoned-up businessmen working in ubiquitous grey bank offices; of secret investment files and precision timing. Of course, the streets are meticulously clean and everything runs like clockwork, but it is also a fun-loving, dynamic and thriving metropolis. It is large enough to offer world-class facilities, but small enough to retain its Swiss charm and 19th-century intimacy.

Most of Zurich's sights fall within a compact, walkable area either side of the Limmat river, which bisects the city centre. The ancient hilly Niederdorf district to the east is a veritable labyrinth of ancient, cobbled lanes brimming with trendy bars, cafés and quirky shops. To the west, the Altstadt (Old Town) contains many of the city's finest historic buildings, and broad, leafy Bahnhofstrasse counts among the world's most sophisticated shopping boulevards. The newly trendy former industrial quarter of Zurich West reflects the city's radical change in recent years, while the lake, with its beautiful grassy parks and lakeside promenades, is framed by majestic, snow-capped mountains.

Located at the heart of Europe, today's Zurich cleverly combines the trams and architecture of Vienna, the waterways of Amsterdam, the street café society of Paris and the cobbled old-town atmosphere of Stockholm into one delightful city. Although not the nation's political capital, this heady mix – together with a world-class art and music scene, the most luxurious shopping in Europe and the infectious *joie de vivre* of its people – demonstrates the city's position as Switzerland's spiritual centre.

When to go

SEASONS & CLIMATE

The city has four distinct seasons, each with a different appeal. Spring (March–May) is a lovely time to visit, before the summer crowds, and when the sweet-scented blossoms of the lime trees on Bahnhofstrasse are in bloom. The weather is mild but it can be rainy. Summer (June–August) is the perfect time to come, when the weather is at its finest and sunniest, although the city is at its busiest. The average summer temperature is around 22°C (71°F) and rarely rises above 30°C (86°F), and the humidity level is pleasant. A dip in the Limmat river or the lake is always refreshing on warm days and balmy evenings. Autumn (September–November) is another popular time, with plenty of crisp, clear, sunny days. The city is quieter and there are excellent bargains in the shops.

○ Zürchers spill on to the streets during the summer

During winter (December–February), once the thermometer falls below 0°C (32°F), the city is covered with a sugar-like sprinkling of snow. It is a magical time, with shop windows elaborately decorated and fairy lights illuminating the streets. However, the temperature usually ranges from a chilly −2°C (28°F) to just 4°C (39°F) by day (and it's even colder at night), so wrap up warmly.

ANNUAL EVENTS

February–March
ZüriCarneval The first major festival of the year is this wild carnival during Lent, with parades, fancy-dress, street entertainment and fireworks in the Niederdorf. ⓦ www.zurichcarneval.ch

April
Sechseläuten (Six o'Clock Bells) marks the end of winter, when the working day traditionally ended with the 18.00 church bells rather than at nightfall. The first ringing of the season celebrates the arrival of spring. A Procession of the Guilds (Zug der Zünfte) winds through the streets, involving around 7,000 participants, 500 horses, music ensembles and carriages. At 18.00 sharp, the guildsmen gallop round a giant bonfire by the lake and light the Böögg, a snowmanlike figure made of straw and fireworks, who represents winter. It is said that the faster his head explodes, the better the summer will be.

June–July
The Zurich Festival is one of Europe's top festivals, with an extensive programme of opera, music, theatre and cultural exhibitions throughout the city. ⓦ www.zuercher-festspiele.ch

July

Live at Sunset is the city's biggest open-air music festival. It takes place at the Dolder Eisbahn, on a hill with a magnificient view, and runs over two weeks. Previous line-ups have included such stars as Diana Ross and Crowded House. Ⓦ www.liveatsunset.ch

August

Street Parade In mid-August, nearly a million party-goers take to the streets for the colourful techno parade, with dancing day and night. Bigger than London's Notting Hill Carnival, it is Europe's largest annual street party. Ⓦ www.streetparade.ch

Theater Spektakel Held during the second half of August, the open-air, lakeside Theater Spektakel is among Europe's leading contemporary performing arts festivals. Ⓦ www.theaterspektakel.ch

September

The Knabenschiessen is one of the oldest events: a shooting competition for teenagers on the Albisgütli, followed by the largest three-day fair in Switzerland. Ⓦ www.knabenschiessen.ch

September–October

Zurich Film Festival Founded in 2005, the Zurich Film Festival has already become one of Europe's most important newcomers – within three years, the number of visitors shot to 27,000. With its red carpet and Hollywood stars, it rivals the traditional International Film Festival in Locarno. Ⓦ www.zurichfilmfestival.org

November

Expovina is the world's biggest wine-tasting show. It takes place aboard 12 boats on the lake and is a wonderful opportunity to taste some little-known Swiss wines. Ⓦ www.expovina.ch

December
During Advent, there are plenty of Christmas concerts and the aromas of gingerbread and *glühwein* (a type of mulled wine) fill the air. (The one at the Hauptbahnhof is Europe's largest covered Christmas market.) One of the loveliest Christmas festivities is the Lichterschwimmen, when floating candles are launched from the Rathausbrücke into the river.

The new year is welcomed in with great revelry and dazzling fireworks by the lake at the nation's largest New Year's Eve party. Ⓦ www.silvesterzauber.ch

PUBLIC HOLIDAYS
New Year's Day 1 Jan
New Year's celebrations 2 Jan
Good Friday 10 Apr 2009; 2 Apr 2010; 22 Apr 2011
Easter Monday 13 Apr 2009; 5 Apr 2010; 25 Apr 2011
Ascension Day 21 May 2009; 13 May 2010; 2 June 2011
Whit Monday 1 June 2009; 24 May 2010; 13 June 2011
Bundesfeier (Swiss National Day) 1 Aug
Christmas Day 25 Dec
Boxing Day 26 Dec

Offices and stores are closed on national holidays (except at the Hauptbahnhof and the airport).

Dada

It may seem surprising that the outlandish, deliberately nonsensical Dada art movement was founded here in neutral, bourgeois Zurich. However, the city had long been a centre of artistic and liberal thought, attracting such scholars as Lenin, Jung, Joyce and Mann. Neutrality during World War I made Zurich a refuge for dissidents, and so Dadaism was founded in 1916 at Cabaret Voltaire (see page 84), a popular rendezvous for writers, painters and musicians. A rebellious anti-war movement and the very antithesis of conformity, it rejected the prevailing oppressive, materialistic standards in art by promoting a new 'anti-art'. The main exponents of the movement in Zurich included Hugo Ball, Tristan Tzara, Hans Arp and Emmy Hennings. Over the years, Dadaism gained support through public gatherings, discussion groups, readings and theatrical performances at Cabaret Voltaire. By 1920 the movement had reached its peak, and its influence reached beyond the visual and literary arts into 'Dada music', created by such composers as Erwin Schulhoff and Hans Heusser.

But Dadaism was not without its critics. A reviewer from the *American Art News* described it as 'the sickest, most paralyzing and most destructive thing that has ever originated from the brain of man'. Years later, even Dada artists described the movement as 'nihilistic... a phenomenon bursting forth in the midst of the post-war economic and moral crisis... a systematic work of destruction and demoralisation... embracing anarchy and the irrational'.

◓ *Cabaret Voltaire is home to the Dadaist movement*

When World War I ended in 1918, many of the Zurich Dadaists returned to promote the movement in their home countries. Ironically, Dadaism went on to influence later, more positive art movements including Surrealism, Pop Art and Fluxus. Cabaret Voltaire fell into disrepair until it was occupied by a group claiming to be neo-Dadaists in 2002. After their eviction, the space reopened in 2004 as a museum dedicated to the history of Dada in Zurich.

History

Zurich's history dates back to 15 BC when a Roman customs post was established on the river on the site now called Lindenhof. They called it Turicum. The Romans built Zurich's first stone buildings and established a harbour and grapevines here. Around 250 people lived at Turicum, and you can see the remains of the ancient Roman baths through a metal grating in Thermengasse in the Altstadt. The Romans eventually withdrew from Zurich in 401 AD, to make way for the Franks and the Alemans. In 1218, Zurich was eventually recognized as a free city and was placed under the authority of the Holy Roman Emperor. To celebrate, the people of Zurich destroyed the Carolingian castle, using it as a quarry, and built the city's first Rathaus (town hall) on the banks of the Limmat river.

In 1336, nobleman Rudolf Brun, with the help of local craftsmen, ousted the city council from the Rathaus and founded the Constitution of the Guilds, thereby giving the city's artisans and traders economic and political power for several centuries. Brun made himself mayor and, during his rule, Zurich joined the Swiss Confederation in 1351 as the capital city of the canton of Zurich. The guilds remain active in society today.

During the Middle Ages, the Fraumünster was built as a convent for noblewomen, and the abbess was granted the right to hold markets, collect tolls and mint money. The Grossmünster was constructed, according to legend, by Charlemagne on the spot where Zurich's patron saints, the martyrs Felix and Regula, were buried (see page 79). Huldrych Zwingli, the first priest at the Grossmünster, initiated the Reformation from here in 1519.

His motto 'pray and work' was to have a profound effect on Zurich. In the second half of the 19th century, Alfred Escher, a trailblazer of modern Switzerland, built the Hauptbahnhof (main railway station) and founded the Swiss rail network, which revolutionized communications and made Zurich the nation's main transportation, research and business hub. It remained the country's political capital until 1848, when that honour was transferred to Bern.

Today Zurich remains the Swiss economic capital (half of the nation's income is generated here) and a major international financial centre. Many of the major Swiss banks have their headquarters here and it is home to the world's fourth-ranked stock market (after New York, Tokyo and London) and the largest gold bullion market. Combine this wealth and business prowess with a strong artistic and intellectual tradition, and a recent boom in gastronomy, dance clubs and popular culture and it is not surprising that Zurich is considered to be one of the most stylish cities in Europe.

◆ *View over the rooftops of historic Zurich*

Lifestyle

Ever since the 1980s, when the Wohlgroth community squat gained notoriety by erecting a huge imitation railway station sign to greet inbound trains to the Hauptbahnhof, which read 'Zu Reich' ('too rich') rather than 'Zurich', people have been joking about the city's affluent lifestyle. But it *is* one of Europe's most expensive cities. The streets are not lined with gold, but there's plenty of it in the city vaults and, of the million or so people living in the canton of Zurich, a disproportionate number are millionaires.

Zurich is Switzerland's largest city, spread across 93 sq km (36 sq miles), and the city itself has a population of around 330,000. This has declined recently as more young people choose to live in the countryside and commute to work. Only six per cent of Zürchers live in their own homes. The rest live in rented accommodation, as is the trend throughout Switzerland. Zurich is an important university city, with over 30,000 students in town, and foreigners have increased in recent years, now representing a quarter of the population. This has also resulted in greater religious freedom. Most Zürchers speak a form of German called *Schwyzerdütsch* (Schweizer-Deutsch in standard German), with its own unique vocabulary, grammar and syntax.

Many Swiss stereotypes reign supreme here: everything runs like clockwork; everyone eats copious amounts of cheese and chocolate; the infamous 'gnomes' (as the British like to call Zurich's bankers) abound; and its citizens are generally law-abiding, efficient, hard-working, clean-living, polite and welcoming to visitors. Indeed, Zurich's hospitality is second to none, and

75 per cent of employees work in the service sector. But in recent years the laws have relaxed and so have the Zürchers. They work hard but they also play hard. The Swiss have access to a great health service, per capita earnings that are among the highest in the world and an outstanding education system. The local lifestyle is admired – and even envied – across the globe. It therefore comes as no surprise that, for five years running, Switzerland's 'little big city' has been voted the world's number one place to live for quality of life.

● *Despite their reputation Zürchers know how to relax*

Culture

For centuries, Zurich has had a strong artistic and intellectual tradition. It has long been a centre of liberal thought, attracting such scholars as Joyce, Mann, Jung, Lenin and Wagner. In 1916 the avant-garde Dadaist movement (see page 14) was born in the Niederdorf when a group of intellectuals rebelled against traditional artistic expression. Ever since, Zurich has been one of the global hubs of contemporary art, along with New York and London, and boasts more than 100 art galleries. Artistic excellence is maintained at the Kunsthaus, the city's foremost gallery, with its impressive collection of paintings and sculptures by Swiss and international masters, predominantly from the 19th and 20th centuries. The Migros Museum of Contemporary Art keeps abreast of the very latest trends, while the reopening of Cabaret Voltaire in 2004 marked the start of a brand new Dada era.

Zurich is also home to the largest number of museums in Switzerland and has more than 50 attractions revealing every aspect of Zürcher history and lifestyle, from toys to tourism. However, none provides better insight into local life than the Schweizerisches Landesmuseum (Swiss National Museum) with its remarkable and extensive collections spanning pre-history and the present day.

Visitors can enjoy concerts and music festivals throughout the year, ranging from small-scale open-air affairs to blockbuster pop events at the Hallenstadion. Opera is world-class, with performances from September to May in the celebrated Opernhaus. During summer months the lakeside open-air cinema is always hugely popular.

The Schweizerisches Landesmuseum charts the history of the Swiss people

Zurich is also undergoing a subcultural revolution, largely due to the re-invention of the formerly industrialised Züri-West district. New life has taken root within the old factory buildings, which now house a wide variety of hip bars and nightclubs. Best-known is the trendy Schiffbau, an alternative venue for Zurich's main theatre. And the world-renowned techno Street Parade (see page 12), with 24-hour dancing in the streets, is now Europe's largest annual street party.

Zurich wears its history on its sleeve through its eclectic mix of architecture, from the photogenic, ancient buildings of the Altstadt, painted in ice-cream shades, to the city's immaculately restored guildhalls flanking the Limmat river, which provide rare insights into bygone city life. Le Corbusier's pavilion by the shores of the lake has left a legacy of 20th-century innovation while, more recently, the converted industrial spaces of Züri-West are supreme examples of post-modern industrial architecture.

For an excellent cultural overview of the city, consider a **guided cycle tour** (Ⓦ www.zurichbybike.ch) or, if you're really brave, a **Ghost Walk** (Ⓦ www.ghostwalk.ch), which delves into the city's past history to find its 'ghosts, ghouls and things that go yodel in the night'!

 Ornate dome of the Grossmünster

Shopping

From beautifully hand-crafted Swiss-made articles through to international luxury labels, shopping in Zurich inspires the fashion-conscious, delights lovers of tradition and never fails to excite souvenir hunters.

The main shopping district occupies a square kilometre at the heart of the city. This area contains everything, from Switzerland's most sophisticated department stores, tiny boutiques and quirky specialist shops to the haute couture of the world-famous shopping mile, the Bahnhofstrasse. While the vaults of gold that power Switzerland's financial centre lie beneath Bahnhofstrasse, at street level the affluent, fur-clad locals are happy to admire the opulent window displays and splash out on the designer clothes, watches, jewellery and chocolates of Zurich's most celebrated boutiques.

The 'in' districts of Sihl and Zurich West specialise in small, trend-setting boutiques, selling everything imaginable whether you're after interior design prototypes or funky shirts for men. Niederdorf contains a multitude of interior design shops and galleries, while the artisan quarter at Schipfe offers treasure troves of antiquities. The city enjoys a flourishing art trade, especially along the Rämistrasse 'art mile'.

Not only does Zurich offer stylish international brand names, it also presents its own urban labels, including Freitag bags (made from recycled truck tarpaulins), street-, beach- and snow-wear with urban attitude from Alprausch, effortlessly fashionable designer shirts by local designer Edo Popken, and sumptuous silk accessories at Fabric Frontline. There is also a bewildering choice of Swiss-made skis and snowboards, jewellery and watches. The finest local handicrafts can be found at Schweizer Heimatwerk. Failing that, there are plenty of nostalgic souvenir shops with amusing collections of beer steins, music boxes, Swiss knives, fondue pots, cuckoo clocks and cow bells...

Gourmets will enjoy the lavish international delicatessens at the Globus and Jelmoli department stores and the local fruit

△ *Chocolate lovers will feel like kids in a sweet shop in Zurich*

USEFUL SHOPPING PHRASES

What time do the shops open/close?
Um wieviel Uhr öffnen/schließen die Geschäfte?
Oom veefeel oor erffnen/shleessen dee geshefter?

How much is this?
Wieviel kostet das?
Veefeel kostet das?

Can I try this on?
Kann ich das anprobieren?
Can ikh das anprobeeren?

My size is ...
Ich habe Größe ...
Ikh haber grerser ...

I'll take this one, thank you
Ich nehme das, danke schön
Ikh neymer das, danker shern

This is too large/too small/too expensive
Es ist zu groß/zu klein/zu teuer
Es ist tsu gross/tsu kline/tsu toyer

and vegetable market at Bürkliplatz on Tuesday and Friday morning (which becomes a flea market on Saturdays). And don't even think of leaving Zurich without buying some chocolate, as it is *the* speciality here. It's hard to miss such celebrated chocolate shops as Sprüngli and Teuscher, with their mouth-watering window displays. Cheese is perhaps Switzerland's most famous export, and several specialist cheese shops offer everything from delicious mountain goats' cheeses to the runniest of *raclette* cheeses.

Eating & drinking

The food scene in Zurich has never been as exciting as it is now, with trendy eateries and world-class restaurants burgeoning throughout the city. There are now nearly 2,000 bars, cafés and restaurants serving a bewildering range of culinary delicacies from around the world, and a remarkable 400 of these serve guests outdoors in mild weather.

Whatever your taste and budget, Zurich has just the right eatery for you, from noodle bars, sausage stands and beer cellars to innovative gourmet temples inside former factory walls, lakeside fish restaurants and traditional guildhall establishments serving delicious Zurich specialities. Undoubtedly the most unusual dining experience is at Blinde Kuh (see page 91), the first restaurant in the world to be run by blind people, where you eat in total darkness. For a special occasion, Petermann's Kunststuben (see page 113) in nearby Küsnacht is Switzerland's top restaurant.

Traditional Swiss food is simple and hearty, relying heavily on dairy produce, and includes such humble mountain cuisine as *rösti* (crispy, fried, grated potato), cheese and meat fondues, *Älpler Magrone* (macaroni cheese served with bacon, onions,

---

PRICE CATEGORIES
The ratings used in this book indicate the typical cost of a three-course meal for one person without drinks.
£ up to CHF 25   ££ CHF 25–75   £££ over CHF 75

● *Backstreet café in Niederdorf*

puréed apples and cinnamon) and *raclette* (melted cheese piled high on new potatoes, gherkins and pickled onions). The neighbouring countries of Austria, Germany, Italy and France have also influenced the local cooking, which in Zurich is frequently meat-heavy due to its proximity to Germany. And recently other world cuisines have gained a foothold, with fusion cuisine all the rage in the city's more fashionable restaurants. Vegetarian restaurants are also on the increase.

Zurich's culinary identity comes largely from its location on Lake Zurich. Its cuisine mixes typical country specialities with some excellent fish dishes too, including such delicacies as lake trout, bream, perch and anglerfish. The city's signature dish, however, is *Züri Gschnetzlets* (Swiss-German for *geschnetzeltes Kalbfleisch nach Zürcherart*, veal in a cream and mushroom sauce).

Look out also for *Leberknodli* (liver dumplings), potato croquettes, *Apfelkuechli* (fried apple slices), *Birchermüsli* (a delicious muesli, fruit and yoghurt mixture, generally eaten as a daytime snack or a light supper) and the ubiquitous *Apfelstrudel* (apple strudel), all commonplace on Zürcher menus.

Fine dining and fine wine go hand in hand in Zurich and there is no shortage of excellent Swiss wine to try. The nation's best come from Valais and include *Fendant* (dry white) and *Dôle* (a smooth red). Zurich's vineyards are located mainly on the 'Gold Coast' of the lake's eastern shore. Look out for *Räuschling*, produced with exclusively Zürcher grapes, and local *Schiterberger* and *Gamaret* reds. For spirits, try *Schnapps*, *Kirsch* (cherry spirit), or *Xellent*, a new triple-distilled vodka made with high-quality Swiss rye and alpine glacier water.

EATING OUT

Eating out is very popular in Zurich and so it is advisable to make a reservation. In cafés, tea rooms, beer halls and less expensive restaurants, table sharing is common. Food is typically served 12.00–14.00 and 18.00–21.00 (22.00 at weekends).

By law restaurants have to display their menus and prices outside, so the price you see is the price you pay (it already includes a service charge of 15 per cent), and tipping is therefore not normally necessary. However, locals often round up the bill. The *Tagesmenu* (menu of the day), usually comprising two or even three courses, can be excellent value.

USEFUL DINING PHRASES

I would like a table for ... people, please
Ich möchte ein Tisch für ... Personen, bitte
Ikh merkhter ine teesh foor ... perzohnen, bitter

Waiter/waitress!	**May I have the bill, please?**
Herr Ober/Frau Kellnerin!	Die Rechnung, bitte?
Hair ohber/frow kell-nair-in!	*Dee rekhnung, bitter?*

I am a vegetarian. Does this contain meat?
Ich bin Vegetarier (Vegetarierin fem.). Enthält das hier Fleisch?
*Ish bin veggetaareer (veggetaareerin). Enthelt dass
heer flyshe?*

Where is the toilet (restroom), please?
Wo sind die Toiletten, bitte?
Voo zeent dee toletten, bitter?

If a picnic lunch is more your style, make a beeline for the fabulous delicatessens in the basements of the Jelmoli and Globus department stores, the fruit and vegetable market at Bürkliplatz (Tuesday and Friday mornings), and local bakeries and cheese shops to stock up on provisions. The most popular picnic venue is the grassy lakeside but, for the energetic, the top of Uetliberg (Uetli Mountain) is undoubtedly the prime spot.

Entertainment & nightlife

Forget yodelling, alp-horns and other types of traditional Swiss entertainment. Zurich is considerably less conservative than it was 15 years ago and nights are now long and sophisticated with over 500 cool, stylish bars, clubs and discos to choose from, many in the Niederdorf and Züri-West quarters. Weekends begin on Thursdays and the city's flamboyant club scene caters to all tastes, although Latin, Techno and House beats take centre stage at present. That said, compared with people in other major European cities, most Zürchers are not night owls. Only a handful party till dawn, and many of the nightspots close down around 01.00 or 02.00 (later at weekends).

In the city centre, sophisticated chill-out bars draw the beautiful people, while most of the gay clubs and bars are located in the Niederdorf quarter, together with a handful of raucous beer cellars. This is also the most likely district to find buskers and other street performers. During summer, when the sun goes down things start to hot up at the city's pools and lidos, with their dreamy open-air bars idyllically located on the banks of the Limmat and the lake. The up-and-coming former industrial quarter of Züri-West has a special buzz about it, with its thriving subculture and its old factories converted into bars, clubs and leisure venues. The city also boasts numerous live music haunts, ranging from mellow, intimate jazz bars and witty oom-pah bands in beer cellars to huge rock and pop arenas, featuring artists from all over the world.

On the cultural front, Zurich offers a prestigious programme of performing arts and cultural events throughout the year. The main venue for classical music is the impressive Tonhalle with its superb acoustics, while the opera and ballet productions at the Opernhaus enjoy a world-wide reputation. Throughout the year, chamber concerts and recitals are staged in churches and museums, and in summer you'll find performances in some of the city parks.

The city's theatre programme is unlikely to appeal to visitors, unless you speak German, in which case there is the full spectrum on offer, from classical to avant-garde and even a **puppet theatre for children** (Ⓦ www.theater-stadelhofen.ch). Cinema, however, is a different matter, with most screenings shown in the original

🔺 *The Zurich Opera House hosts world-class productions*

LISTINGS

The best source of local entertainment listings is the daily newspaper *Tages Anzeiger* (available from newsstands), whose weekly 'Züritipp' section previews cinema, theatre, music and nightlife. There are also listings in the daily *Neue Zürcher Zeitung* (NZZ), while the monthly magazine *Swiss News* (available in newsagents and English bookshops) documents what's on in English. The Tourist Office is an excellent source of cultural knowledge, with its useful *Zurich Events* leaflet, or pick up the nightlife booklets *Wakeup Agenda* or *Zurich Night Guide* in various bars around town. For further, detailed nightlife info, grab one of the free papers (*20 Minuten* or *Blick am Abend*) found in boxes at tram and train stations. And check out the online event guide at Ⓦ www.zueritipp.ch

version with subtitles. Open-air cinema is especially popular in summer, when giant screens are erected by the lake and river. Check the website Ⓦ www.orangefestival.ch for further info.

Tickets are best purchased from the relevant box office at each venue. Alternatively, book by phone or via the internet at Ⓦ www.ticketcorner.com, www.starticket.ch or www.tictec.ch. The **Hauptbahnhof Tourist Office**'s cultural information desk (Ⓣ 044 215 40 00 Ⓦ www.zuerich.com) and the department stores Jelmoli (see page 73) and **Migros** (Ⓐ Löwenstr. 31 Ⓦ www.migros.ch) offer advance bookings for theatre, musicals, opera, classical concerts, cabaret and other events.

Sport & relaxation

PARTICIPATION SPORTS

One of the joys of Zurich is its proximity to nature, with the river, the lake and the majestic mountains all on the doorstep. Zürchers enjoy a healthy outdoor lifestyle, including the following:

Boating

Hire a pedalo or a motorboat from various locations around the lake (see page 104).

Cycling

Throughout the summer season, Zürirollt offers free bike hire from stalls at the Hauptbahnhof, Globus-City and the Opera House (for details see page 55). ⓦ www.zuerirollt.ch

In-line skating

Tour the lake, and join the infamous **Monday Night Skate** (❸ Departs from Bürklipl. ⓦ www.nightskate.ch ⓛ Every second Monday, spring–autumn) or the Swiss In-line Cup in June, the world's largest in-line marathon.

Swimming

Take a dip in the lake, the river or one of the many pools and lidos around the city (ⓦ www.badi-info.ch/zueri-badis.html). Alternatively, head to Alpamare (see page 108), the largest indoor water-park in Europe.

Volleyball

There's beach volleyball during summer at the Flussbad Obere Letten lido.

Walking

Stroll along the lake, climb Uetliberg (see page 67) or hike in the wooded hills of the picture-postcard Zürcher Oberland region.

Winter sports

It takes just a couple of hours by train to reach some of the country's top ski resorts, such as Davos, Klosters, Flims and Laax. These are all easily accessible by train from the Hauptbahnhof (change in Landquart for Davos and Klosters; Chur for Flims and Laax), as are some smaller, lesser-known resorts, including Hoch Ybrig (see page 113) and Flums (change in Ziegelbrücke or Sargans), all within 1½ hours by train from Zurich.

SPECTATOR SPORTS

Zurich's sporting events attract visitors from around the world. Many take place at the **Hallenstadion** (ⓦ www.hallenstadion.ch Ⓝ S-Bahn: Bahnhof Oerlikon). Tickets are available from the box office or online at ⓦ www.ticketcorner.com

Football

Zurich is the FIFA headquarters and occasionally hosts international football matches.

Freestyle.ch

An event showcasing all the latest tricks and stunts in

snowboarding, free-skiing and skateboarding. ⓐ Landiwiese
Ⓦ www.freestyle.ch

Ice hockey

The Swiss team ZSC Lions plays at the Hallenstadion. Matches
are played throughout the winter season and are always a thrill
to watch. ⓐ Hallenstadion Ⓦ www.zsc-lions.ch

Ice skating

Art on Ice is a glitzy show performed by international figure
skaters in February. ⓐ Hallenstadion Ⓦ www.artonice.ch

Marathon

The international Zurich Marathon, the largest in Switzerland,
runs in April. Ⓦ www.zurichmarathon.com

🔺 *Runners in the Zurich Marathon*

Accommodation

Swiss hospitality is world-renowned and Zurich has over 120 hotels ranging from 5-star deluxe and chic boutique hotels to simple guesthouses and youth hostels. Finding accommodation can be difficult, so try to reserve in advance.

As a general rule, the closer to the lake, the pricier the accommodation. The atmospheric Altstadt also commands high prices for its traditional ambience. More affordable hotels can be found in some of the backstreets, and especially in Niederdorf, although this quarter can be rather lively at night. Some of the cheapest accommodation is in trendy Zurich West.

City Backpacker £ A lively, international atmosphere greets you at this centrally placed youth hostel with private rooms, family rooms, dormitories and self-catering facilities.
🅐 Niederdorfstr. 5 (Niederdorf & beyond) ☎ 044 251 90 15
🅦 www.city-backpacker.ch

Comfort Inn Royal £ Friendly, stylish business accommodation in the city centre. 🅐 Leonhardstr. 6 (Central Zurich) ☎ 044 266 59 59
🅦 www.comfortinn.ch

> **PRICE CATEGORIES**
> The ratings used in this book indicate the typical cost of a double room with breakfast for one night.
> **£** up to CHF 250 **££** CHF 250–400 **£££** over CHF 400

Hirschen £ This clean, simple, family-run guesthouse has been accommodating visitors at the heart of Niederdorf for more than 300 years. ⓐ Niederdorfstr. 13 (Niederdorf & beyond) ⓣ 043 286 33 33 ⓦ www.hirschen-zuerich.ch

Leoneck £ An offbeat, fun choice, decorated in 'Swiss ethno' style. The rooms have original wall paintings by local artists, and there are cow motifs everywhere. Superb value. ⓐ Leonhardstr. 1 (Central Zurich) ⓣ 044 254 22 22 ⓦ www.leoneck.ch

X-TRA £ At the heart of the trendy Züri-West district, this Bauhaus hotel adjoining the city's largest nightclub appeals to a young crowd. ⓐ Limmatstr. 118 (Central Zurich) ⓣ 044 448 15 95 ⓦ www.x-tra.ch

◓ *The striking curves of the Greulich hotel*

Zürcherhof £ A popular business hotel with budget prices and non-smoking rooms, on the fringe of lively Niederdorf. ⓐ Zähringerstr. 21 (Central Zurich) ⓣ 044 269 44 44 ⓦ www.hotelzuercherhof.ch

Greulich ££ A boutique hotel in a renovated industrial building, with minimalist furnishings and neutral colour schemes by Jean Pfaff, a Swiss artist known for his monochromatic art. The 18 rooms are clustered around inner courtyard gardens with birch trees and Zen-like water pools. ⓐ Herman Greulich-Str. 56 (Central Zurich) ⓣ 043 243 42 43 ⓦ www.greulich.ch

Helmhaus ££ A friendly Niederdorf hotel combining traditional hospitality with modern comforts (including Wi-Fi throughout). Ask for a room overlooking the river. ⓐ Schifflände 30 (am Limmatquai, Central Zurich) ⓣ 044 266 95 95 ⓦ www.helmhaus.ch

Hôtel du Théâtre ££ Formerly a German-speaking theatre, this stylish B&B near the Hauptbahnhof offers comfortable accommodation with unusual theatrical decor. ⓐ Seilergraben 69 (Central Zurich) ⓣ 044 267 26 70 ⓦ www.hotel-du-theatre.ch

Lady's First Design Hotel ££ This stucco-fronted 19th-century villa near the lake once accommodated country girls at finishing school. Today, its original features combine with chic, 21st-century decor. Facilities include a wellness centre (for women only) and a fabulous roof terrace. ⓐ Mainaustr. 24 (Central Zurich) ⓣ 044 380 80 10 ⓦ www.ladysfirst.ch ⓝ Tram: 4 (Feldeggstrasse)

Rigihof ££ A Bauhaus-style hotel near the university, with 66 rooms, each dedicated to celebrities once living or working in Zurich, including Max Bill, Carl Jung, Johanna Spyri, and many more. ⓐ Universitätstr. 101 (Central Zurich) ⓣ 044 360 12 07

Romantik Florhof ££ A romantic boutique hotel with just 35 rooms in a former 15th-century merchant's home, in a tranquil, leafy setting near the Kunsthaus. ⓐ Florhofgasse 4 (Central Zurich) ⓣ 044 250 26 26 ⓦ www.florhof.ch

Rössli ££ Ultra-small, stylish and affordable, this is a favourite with hip business travellers. Contemporary white-on-white decor and a charming roof terrace overlooking the old town. ⓐ Rössligasse 7 (Central Zurich) ⓣ 044 256 70 50 ⓦ www.hotelroessli.ch

Rutli ££ A simple, modern hotel at the heart of Niederdorf with unusual, graffiti-style decor. ⓐ Zähringerstr. 43 (Central Zurich) ⓣ 044 254 58 00 ⓦ www.rutli.ch

Seefeld ££ State-of-the-art technology and design are the hallmarks of this trendy hotel, near the opera house, the lake and Bellevue. The bar draws the beautiful people of Zurich and there is also a roof terrace, Wi-Fi access throughout, and a small gym. ⓐ Seefeldstr. 63 (Central Zurich) ⓣ 044 387 41 41 ⓦ www.hotel-seefeld.ch

Seidenhof ££ Just off Bahnhofstrasse, this highly functional yet stylish hotel was once an important centre for the city's silk trade.

Facilities include Wi-Fi and high-speed internet access in all rooms, a minimalist, modern-Asian restaurant and a massage centre for its over-stressed business clientele. ⓐ Sihlstr. 9 (Central Zurich) ⓣ 044 228 75 00 ⓦ www.seidenhof.ch; www.the-massage-therapy.ch

Uto Kulm ££–£££ For a truly tranquil retreat, escape the city bustle and stay in a car-free zone on Uetliberg, the so-called 'Top of Zurich' (see page 67). Design is paramount in this classy, minimalist hotel, with its clever use of fine natural materials, and breathtaking vistas. For that special occasion, you can reserve a luxurious 'romantic' suite: the Tower Suite has a wood-burning stove and a heart-shaped whirlpool bath. ⓐ Uetliberg (Central Zurich) ⓣ 044 457 66 66 ⓦ www.utokulm.ch

Baur au Lac £££ Among Switzerland's grandest hotels, in an unsurpassed location adjoining Bahnhofstrasse and with a private park by the lake, this traditional, family-run hotel has welcomed such luminaries as Wagner, Liszt and Lennon since its opening in 1844. ⓐ Talstr. 1 (Central Zurich) ⓣ 044 220 50 20 ⓦ www.bauraulac.ch

Widder £££ Just off Bahnhofstrasse, this striking, luxury hotel in the Altstadt consists of ten ancient interlinked townhouses, cleverly fused together by Zurich artist Tilla Theuss. Think ancient frescoes, exposed bricks and wooden beams brilliantly juxtaposed with glass and chrome, plus a roof-top terrace with spectacular views, and a chic jazz bar. ⓐ Rennweg 7 (Central Zurich) ⓣ 044 224 25 26 ⓦ www.widderhotel.ch

THE BEST OF ZURICH

Zurich is compact, and both easy and enjoyable to explore on foot, thanks to its beautiful lake, elegant streets, graceful spires and its maze of cobbled alleyways fringing the river. Most main sights lie in and around the car-free Altstadt and Niederdorf. The remainder are easily accessible by tram.

TOP 10 ATTRACTIONS

- **Schweizerisches Landesmuseum** Make this fascinating museum your first port of call. Once you have a grasp of the nation's colourful history, walks around town are all the more rewarding (see page 99)

- **Kunsthaus** Switzerland's top art gallery spans the centuries from the Middle Ages to the present, but specialises in 19th- and 20th-century Swiss art (see page 86)

- **Fraumünster** Renowned for its five world-famous stained-glass windows by Chagall, which together represent a lavish fusion of colour and ethereality (see page 65)

- **Bahnhofstrasse** The city's main thoroughfare, a shoppers' paradise and the most overt manifestation of the country's wealth (see page 61)

- **Lake Zurich** An idyllic setting for boating, swimming, walking, picnicking or simply relaxing on the grassy banks (see pages 104–115)

- **Niederdorf** This ancient quarter, distinguished by its picturesque cobbled streets, tiny specialist shops, bars and restaurants, is especially atmospheric by night (see pages 78–93)

- **Grossmünster** The city's cathedral and the birthplace of the Swiss Reformation. Climb the tower for the best aerial views of the city (see page 79)

- **Altstadt** The city's most charming quarter, with its steep, cobbled lanes, beautiful mansions and tranquil, shady squares (see page 60)

- **Migros Museum für Gegenwartskunst** Extraordinary paintings, sculpture and photography by the top trend-setters in contemporary art, housed in a former brewery (see page 98)

- **Uetliberg** Affectionately called the 'Top of Zurich', Uetli Mountain has sensational 360° views of the city, the lake and the Alps (see page 67)

▼ *Ornamental beer steins*

Suggested itineraries

HALF-DAY: ZURICH IN A HURRY

If you only have a few hours, start at the Hauptbahnhof and stroll along the celebrated Bahnhofstrasse, admiring the glittering window displays. Stop for coffee at Sprüngli in Paradeplatz before heading down to the lake to glimpse the city's snow-capped, mountainous backdrop. Head back along the river to visit Fraumünster with its dazzling stained-glass windows by Chagall, or the Grossmünster on the east bank of the Limmat, before enjoying a snack in a typical Zurich café.

1 DAY: TIME TO SEE A LITTLE MORE

After you have completed the recommended half-day sightseeing, add a museum visit to your itinerary. The Schweizerisches Landesmuseum provides a fascinating historical background to the city, while the Kunsthaus is the city's finest gallery. Spend the rest of the day exploring Niederdorf, dipping into its delightful quirky boutiques, and its trendy cafés and bars, before enjoying a sumptuous dinner in one of the ancient guildhall restaurants.

2–3 DAYS: TIME TO SEE MUCH MORE

The extra days provide plenty of time to explore the lake. Stroll along the east bank and take time out to watch the world go by. Then take a boat trip for a new perspective of the city. Alternatively, take in another museum – modern art lovers in particular will enjoy the Migros Museum – or climb to the summit of Uetliberg, Zurich's very own mountain. You'll also have time to eat some chocolate, buy some souvenirs, and check out the city's nightlife.

LONGER: ENJOYING ZURICH TO THE FULL

A longer stay enables you to soak up the café culture of Niederdorf, appreciate the relaxed yet efficient lifestyle of the Zürchers, and top up your tan in the city's legendry lidos. You should also take at least one trip out of town (see pages 104–126).

⬤ The Grossmünster dominates the Zurich skyline

Something for nothing

Strapped for cash in one of the world's most expensive cities? Don't worry! There are plenty of sights and attractions to amuse you, without placing demands on your wallet.

Art aficionados on a budget need not be disappointed in Zurich, as many of the museums and galleries are free, including the Helmhaus (see page 85), the Museum Schweizer Hotellerie & Tourismus (Swiss Hostelry & Tourism Museum, see page 86) and the Spielzeugmuseum (Toy Museum, see page 134). Even the beautiful Botanischer Garten, the pièce de résistance of all the city parks and gardens, is free (see page 78).

For a taste of historic Zurich, explore the Altstadt, where the hilly, cobbled streets are lined with romantic, shuttered houses, many painted in pastel shades and adorned with cascading geraniums. Don't forget to admire the interiors of the magnificent churches (most are free). Then soak up the atmosphere and people-watch in the sociable Niederdorf quarter (see pages 78–93). Better still, why not explore the city on a free hire bike (see page 55)?

Zurich is a shoppers' paradise and, even if you can't afford the shops' contents, you should certainly spend time admiring their window displays, particularly in the grand Bahnhofstrasse.

On a fine day, there is nothing more enjoyable than walking along the quaysides of the Limmat and the lake. The lake draws visitors and locals alike to its shores to relax, snooze, sunbathe or simply watch the world go by. In summer months, it's even warm enough for swimming. Stroll along its western shore and before long you'll be out in the countryside. Or, if you're feeling really energetic, climb to the top of Uetliberg for stunning views of the city and the Alps and a picnic spot to take your breath away.

If you're lucky, you may experience one of Zurich's 'free' street parties (see pages 11–12), should your visit coincide with one of the annual celebrations for Carnival, Sechseläuten or New Year, or the massive Street Parade in August.

Finally, who says everything in Switzerland is expensive? Zurich serves free drinks... from its 1,200 ornamental drinking fountains! They all provide free water to quench your thirst after a long, hot, 'free' day of sightseeing.

🔺 *The Helmhaus holds free exhibitions of cutting-edge art*

When it rains

The bad news is that it can rain in Zurich at any time of year. But the good news is that there are plenty of attractions catering for all ages and interests to keep you amused in the heaviest downpour or even in a winter snowstorm.

For starters, why not take a guided Classic Trolley Tour of the city? It's a great way to get your bearings, to learn a little about

● Hop on a Trolley for a whistle-stop tour of the city

the history and lifestyle of the Zürchers, and to sightsee under cover.

Avoid the showers by visiting one of over a hundred museums and galleries catering for all ages and interests, from high-brow contemporary art to toy, chocolate and watch museums. At the Kunsthaus, Zurich's premier gallery, the sun-drenched Impressionist landscapes of Monet, Cézanne and Van Gogh are bound to brighten the rainiest of days. Or seek refuge from the elements in the city's magnificent churches. Fraumünster is best known for its stunning Chagall stained-glass windows, while Grossmünster, the city's cathedral, is austere but grandiose.

Zurich's shopping ranks among the best in the world, and there are several large department stores in and around Bahnhofstrasse (including Globus, Jelmoli, Grieder and Manor) to occupy any keen shopper for hours.

Children young and old will love a visit to Zoo Zurich (see page 83) even in the rain; there are numerous indoor displays, which include a spectacular rainforest with its own tropical microclimate. Alpamare (see page 108), the largest covered aquatic park in Europe, with its massive tangle of slides, whirlpools and thermal pools, is also an ideal family outing when it's wet.

If that sounds too energetic, join locals for the fine Zurich tradition of coffee and cake mid-morning, mid-afternoon, or indeed at any time. Sprüngli at Paradeplatz or Café Schober in Niederdorf are two of the best-loved venues. And in the evening, take your pick of trendy designer bars, cosy, old-fashioned beer cellars, or intimate, candle-lit traditional pubs.

On arrival

TIME DIFFERENCES

Swiss clocks follow Central European Time (CET). During Daylight Saving Time (end Mar–end Oct), the clocks are put forward one hour.

ARRIVING

By air

Zurich's **Kloten Airport** (ⓦ www.zurich-airport.com), Switzerland's largest international airport, has excellent facilities and shopping.

The airport is located 11 km (7 miles) north of the city. The 24-hour taxi service to the city centre is expensive (around CHF 50). Alternatively, there is a train every 10 minutes to the Hauptbahnhof (main station), operating 06.00–00.00, which takes 10 minutes and costs around CHF 6. Some hotels offer a direct airport shuttle service.

By rail

The swift, punctual Swiss railway network provides easy access to the city and enjoyable, stress-free excursions further afield. More than 1,900 trains halt at the Hauptbahnhof daily from all over Europe (ticket office ⓛ 05.30–23.15).

By road

Zurich's main **bus station** is located at Sihlquai (ⓐ Ausstellungsstr. 15 ⓞ 044 216 53 39), just behind the Hauptbahnhof. An efficient bus network connects all the main cities in Switzerland and abroad.

Driving in Switzerland is relatively straightforward and Zurich is easily accessed via the N1 from Bern (to the west) or St Gallen (to the east).

FINDING YOUR FEET

Despite first impressions of an ultra-efficient, spick and span city, the pace of life in Zurich is surprisingly relaxed and the people are friendly and happy to help. It's safe with a low crime rate but there are incidents of petty crime, so do take common-sense precautions (see Health, safety & crime, page 130), especially in Zurich West and at the northern end of Niederdorf.

ORIENTATION

The city is divided into districts, each with its own distinctive characteristics. Many quarters are pedestrianised, including Bahnhofstrasse, Zurich's most celebrated shopping boulevard.

● *The Hauptbahnhof, Zurich's main train station*

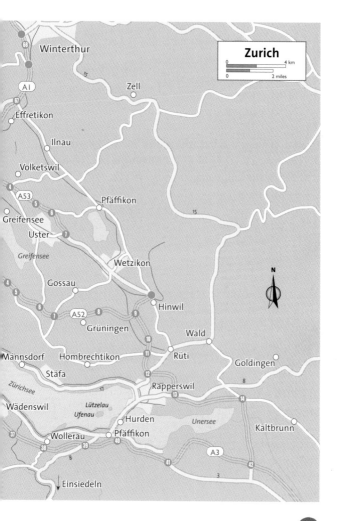

IF YOU GET LOST, TRY ...

Excuse me, do you speak English?
Entschuldigen Sie, sprechen Sie Englisch?
Entshuldigen zee, shprekhen zee english?

Excuse me, is this the right way to the old town/the city centre/the tourist office/the station/the bus station?
Entschuldigung, geht es hier zur Altstadt/zur Stadtmitte/
zur Touristeninformation/zum Bahnhof/zum Busbahnhof?
*Entshuldeegoong, gayt es here tsoor altshtat/tsoor shtatmitter/
zur Touristeninformasion/tsoom baanhof/tsoom busbaanhof?*

Lose yourself in the labyrinth of narrow streets and alleys of the Altstadt (on the west bank of Limmat river) or Niederdorf (on the east bank); there are city maps at the tram stops, and a host of unmissable landmarks, such as the river, the lake, and the spires of the Grossmünster, Fraumünster and St-Peterskirche that help you get your bearings.

GETTING AROUND
Zurich's public transport system is operated by **VBZ Züri-Linie**
(Zurich Public Transport ☎ 0848 988 988 ⊛ www.vbz.ch). The
ticket systems of all public transport in the canton are linked
together, which means you only need one ticket whether you
travel by tram, bus, boat or train.

By tram & bus

The extensive, efficient network of trams and buses runs daily from 05.30 to 00.30. You must buy a ticket before you embark, or you may be fined. Many different types of ticket are available, including a *Kurzstrecke*, valid for a trip of up to four stops, and a *Tageskarte*, which is valid for one day.

By bicycle

Zürirollt (🕐 07.30–21.20 May–Oct Ⓦ www.zuerirollt.ch) offers free bike hire from mid-May–Oct, from small white stands located outside the Hauptbahnhof, Globus-City and the Opera House.

By boat

Zürichsee Schifffahrt (Ⓦ www.zsg.ch) operates lake cruises from Bürkliplatz Pier throughout the year, as well as speciality cruises,

---

ZÜRICHCARD

If you are staying in the city for two or three days and plan to sightsee, consider getting a ZürichCARD, which offers unlimited travel by tram, bus, train, boat, cable-car and funicular, free entry to over 40 museums, and a host of other attractive offers and discounts. Twenty-four and seventy-two hour versions are available and can be purchased from VBZ ticket booths, train stations, the airport, major hotels and the Tourist Office in the Hauptbahnhof. The ticket becomes valid once you stamp it in one of the ticket machines at a transport stop. Ⓦ www.zuerich.com

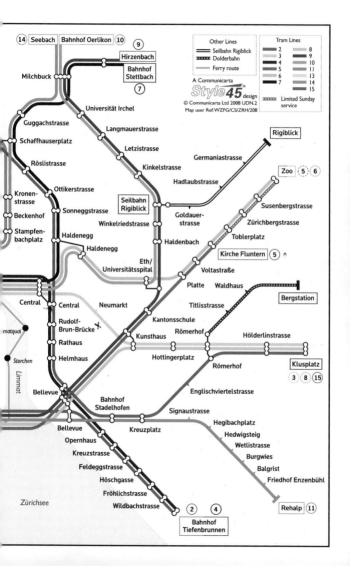

> **DRIVING IN SWITZERLAND**
> *Vignettes* (annual motorway tax discs) cost around CHF 30
> and are available from the **Switzerland Travel Centre** in
> London (☎ 0800 100 200 30 🌐 www.swisstravelsystem.com)
> or from border customs offices, service stations, garages
> and post offices in Switzerland. Failure to display one on
> a motorway can result in a hefty fine.

which include a sunset cruise, a summer brunch boat and a winter
fondue boat. **Limmatschifffahrt** (🌐 www.zvv.ch) plies up Limmat
river from Bürkliplatz Pier to the Landesmuseum twice an hour
from April to October.

By car
There is little need for a car in Zurich, as the public transport
system is so reliable and efficient. City centre parking is scarce
and expensive.

CAR HIRE
It is only worthwhile hiring a car if you are heading out of town
to explore the countryside. There are several hire car companies
at the airport.
Avis ☎ 0848 81 18 18 🌐 www.avis.ch
Budget ☎ 044 813 31 31 🌐 www.budget.com
Europcar ☎ 043 255 56 56 🌐 www.europcar.ch

● *The slender-spired Fraumünster*

Central Zurich

Central Zurich is the district of high finance and elegant shops, centred round the celebrated Bahnhofstrasse, one of Europe's most prestigious streets, where all Zürchers come to promenade and shop. Clinging to the banks of the Limmat river, the neighbouring, car-free Altstadt is the oldest part of town, with its delightful cobbled lanes and luxury boutiques. The entire district is dominated by its spires – the slender green spire of Fraumünster and the graceful spire of St-Peterskirche, featuring the largest clock face in Europe.

SIGHTS & ATTRACTIONS

Altstadt (Old Town)

The early medieval Old Town flanks the Limmat river and is characterized by a cobweb of picturesque lanes, steep cobbled alleyways and hidden sun-splashed squares. The streets are lined with romantic, ancient houses, many adorned with cascading geraniums. Highlights include: Lindenhof, the former Roman customs post; Weinplatz, the oldest market square; Thermengasse, an alley constructed over an excavated Roman bath; Augustinergasse, a street with attractive oriel windows; Münsterhof, the grandest square; and Münzplatz, overlooked by the Augustinerkirche, an austere but beautiful church that was secularized for a while during the Reformation for use as the town's mint. Tram: 6, 7, 11, 13 (Rennweg); Tram: 2, 6, 7, 8, 9, 11, 13 (Paradeplatz)

Bahnhofstrasse

Bahnhofstrasse is reputed to have the most expensive real estate prices in the world. However, it is perhaps best known for its shopping. Indeed, this car-free shopping mile symbolises everything Zurich represents; elegance and prestige, quality, financial prowess and economic diversity. It leads from the Hauptbahnhof (main railway station) to Lake Zurich, and follows the ancient course of the western city wall, past some of the most exclusive jewellers, watchmakers and fashion boutiques in the world.

● *A characteristic Altstadt building*

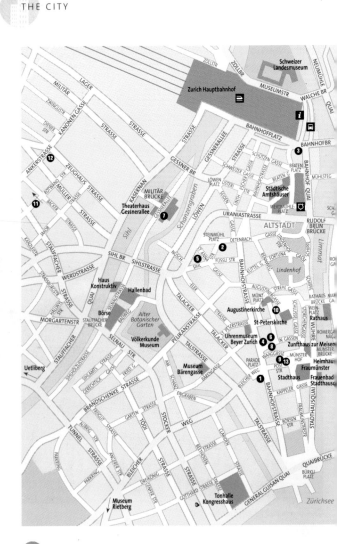

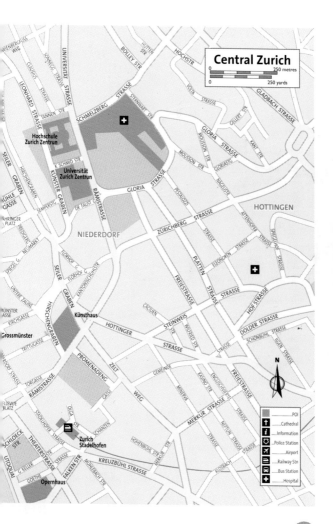

Central Zurich

0 — 250 metres
0 — 250 yards

BOLLEY STR
HOCHSTR
WIENBERGFUSS WEG
SONNEGG STRASSE
UNIVERSITAT STRASSE
CLAUSIS STRASSE
TANNEN STR
LEONHARD STRASSE
SCHMELZBERG STRASSE
STERNWART STR
HUTTEN STR
VOTA STRASSE
GLADBACH STRASSE
GELLERT STR
GLORIA STRASSE
MOUSSON STR
SANT STR
MOUSSON STR
GLORIASTR
Hochschule Zurich Zentrun
SEILER GRABEN
HIRSCHENGRABEN
KUNSTLER GRABEN
K. SCHMID STR
Universität Zurich Zentrun
SEMPERSTR
RAMISTRASSE
DR FAUST STR
GLORIA STRASSE
PASTALOZ
ZURICHBERG STRASSE
HOTTINGEN
MÜHLE GASSE
AHRINGER PLATZ
PRESCOG
NEUMARKT
SPIEGEL G
NIEDERDORF
FLORHOF
FLORHOF G
LANDESMUSEUMSTR
PLATTEN STRASSE
ELEONONEN STR
ATTENHOF STRASSE
BREGELSTRA
MÜNSTER ASSE
UNTERE ZAUNE
KIRCHGASSE
SEILER GRABEN
HIRSCHENGRABEN
Künsthaus
HOTTINGER
CACURN
STEINWEIS
WINFRIED STR
FREISTRASSE
STRASSE
HOF STRASSE
Grossmünster
STRASSE
TRITTLIGASSE
PROMENADENG
ZELT
STRASSE
GEMEINDE
CASINO STR
ENGLISCHER STR
DOLDER STRASSE
SCHONBÜHL STRASSE
TOBELSTRASSE
TEGAN STRASSE
TORGASSE
RAMISTRASSE
WEG
MINERVA
FREISTRASSE
ELLESEVE PLATZ
STADTHOFG
OLGA STR
SCHANZEN
Zurich Stadelhofen
MERKUR STRASSE
NEPTUN STRASSE
SCHLOECK STR
THEATERSTRASSE
FALKEN STR
HOHENBÜHL STR
MERKUR STR
KLOSBACH STRASSE
UTOQUAI
G KELLER
COETHE
Opernhaus
KREUZBÜHL STRASSE
MÜHLEBACH STRASSE

N

Legend:
- POI
- ✝ Cathedral
- 𝒊 Information
- Police Station
- ✈ Airport
- ⬛ Railway Stn
- Bus Station
- ✚ Hospital

A GOLDEN CITY

There's no denying the Swiss are an affluent nation and it's in Zurich that the serious money begins. Most major Swiss banks have their headquarters in and around Paradeplatz, and Zurich is the world's largest gold market. When you stroll up wealthy Bahnhofstrasse you're actually walking on gold. Admittedly, the street is not paved with it but, immediately beneath your feet, the massive bank vaults are full of gold ingots.

Two-thirds of the way along lies Paradeplatz (Parade Square), the scene of a medieval market until the 19th century, when it became the main venue for military processions. Nowadays it is the modern centre of the city, a major tram intersection, and the main location of Sprüngli, the city's most celebrated confectioner. The bars and cafés here offer some of the best people-watching in town.

Bahnhofstrasse ends at Bürkliplatz, the main departure point for boat trips, with majestic views across the lake to the distant snow-capped mountains. ⓐ Bahnhofstr. ⓦ www.bahnhofstrasse-zuerich.ch ⓝ Tram: 6, 7, 11, 13 (Bahnhofstrasse); Tram: 2, 6, 7, 8, 9, 11, 13 (Paradeplatz); Tram: 2, 8, 9, 11 (Bürkliplatz)

Frauenbadi-Stadthausquai

This small, riverside lido is the only surviving example of a typical 19th-century floating lido and it provides an oasis of calm at the heart of the city, open only to women for swimming, massage and relaxation. By night, it becomes the Barfuss Bar, popular with both men and women, but everyone must be 'barefoot', as the name suggests. ⓐ Stadthausquai ⓣ 044 211 95 92 ⓛ Lido: 07.30–19.30 mid-May–mid-Sept (depending on water temperature) ⓝ Tram: 2, 8, 9, 11 (Börsenstrasse). Admission charge

Fraumünster

The main attraction of this elegant church with its slim green spire is the five stained-glass chancel windows created by Marc Chagall in 1970. Each window has its own colour theme; the blue 'Jacob' window, the green 'Christ' window, and the yellow 'Zion' window are on the main wall, flanked by the red 'Prophets' window to the left and the blue 'Law' window to the right.

The church itself is situated beside the river, overlooking the picturesque old town square and former pig market, Münsterhof. The edifice dates from the 13th century, built on the site of an early Benedictine abbey whose crypt has been preserved beneath the church. ⓐ Fraumünsterstr. ⓛ 10.00–18.00 Mon–Sat, 11.15–18.00 Sun, Apr–Oct; 10.00–16.00 Mon–Sat, 11.15–16.00 Sun, Nov–Mar ⓝ Tram: 2, 6, 7, 8, 9, 11, 13 (Paradeplatz)

Limmat (Limmat River)

The city is bisected by the river, which flows from the northern end of Lake Zurich. Its most scenic stretch is from Bahnhofbrücke to Quaibrücke, where the attractive, multi-coloured houses of the historic old town flank both banks. Between these two bridges, four further crossing points (Muhlesteg, Rudolf-Brun-Brücke, Rathausbrücke and Münsterbrücke) unite the east and west banks of the city. The Schipfe, Wuhre and Stadthausquai are especially pleasant for strolling. During summer months cruise vessels ply the river between the Swiss National Museum and the lake.

Lindenhof

The bird's-eye views merit the steep climb to tranquil Lindenhof, the oldest part of Zurich and the original site of the Romans in 15 BC (see page 16). Today this broad, leafy park overlooking the roofs of the Altstadt is an oasis of peace, popular with locals for lunch breaks, and old-timers for *boules* and chess. The surrounding streets contain some of the city's most beautiful medieval wood-framed houses. ⓝ Tram: 6, 7, 11, 13 (Rennweg)

St-Peterskirche (St Peter's Church)

No matter where you are in the city, it's hard to miss St Peter's, as it boasts the largest clock face in Europe, 8.7 m (28.5 ft) in

⬤ *The Münsterbrücke links the east and west banks of the Limmat River*

diameter. The church itself is the city's oldest parish church, founded in the early seventh century, while the tranquil St Peterhofstatt is considered the Altstadt's loveliest square.
ⓐ St Peterhofstatt ⓛ 08.00–18.00 Mon–Fri, 08.00–16.00 Sat
Ⓜ Tram: 6, 7, 11, 13 (Rennweg)

Uetliberg (Uetli Mountain)

Uetliberg is the tallest point in the city, at 871 m (2,857 ft). From here there is a popular two-hour hiking route along a forested mountain ridge, with glorious views over the city, the lake and the Alps. Just 15 minutes from the high-tech, jet-set glamour of the city centre, you can escape to the lush meadows, tinkling cowbells and chocolate-box landscapes that set Switzerland apart. Ⓦ www.uetliberg.ch Ⓜ S-Bahn: Uetliberg

Zürichsee (Lake Zurich)

The 'blue lung' of the city and the fourth largest lake in Switzerland is hugely popular with Zürchers for boating, strolling, swimming, sunbathing, barbecuing or simply chilling out. No trip to Zurich is complete without a mini-cruise to admire the grandiose mansions lining the shores, and Bürkliplatz is the chief departure point for boat trips on the lake. Choose from a variety of year-round excursions ranging from nostalgic paddle-steamer tours to fondue cruises (see page 104).

CULTURE

Haus Konstruktiv (House for Constructive Art)

The Constructive Art Movement was founded in Zurich. Leading exponents Max Bill, Verena Loewensberg, Camille Graeser and Richard Paul Lohse all had their ateliers here, and their abstract art forms, based on geometric principles, came to the fore during World War II. Today, the Foundation for Constructive Art is housed in a former power station on the Sihl river, close to the city centre, and hosts regular temporary exhibitions to promote Constructivist, Concrete and Concept art and design. 🄰 ewz-Unterwerk Selnau, Selnaustr. 25 🄣 044 217 70 80 🅆 www.hauskonstruktiv.ch 🄻 12.00–18.00 Tues, Thur & Fri, 12.00–20.00 Wed, 11.00–18.00 Sat & Sun 🄽 Tram: 8 (Bahnhof Selnau); Tram: 2, 3, 9, 14 (Stauffacher). Admission charge

Museum Bärengasse

The Bärengasse Museum forms part of the Swiss National Museum. Housed in two beautiful baroque houses, it provides a rare insight into Renaissance city life through an appealing collection of furnishings, costumes, coins, musical instruments, maps and portraits of local dignitaries. There is also a small doll museum. 🄰 Bärengasse 20–22 🄣 044 211 17 16 🅆 www.musee-suisse.ch/baerengasse 🄻 10.30–17.00 Tues–Sun, Jan & Feb; 14.00–20.00 Tues, 14.00–18.00 Wed–Sun, Mar–Dec 🄽 Tram: 2, 6, 7, 8, 9, 11, 13 (Paradeplatz). Admission charge

Museum Rietberg

Set in lush parkland, the Rietberg Museum is Switzerland's only gallery for non-European cultures, and boasts an internationally renowned collection of art from Asia, Africa, America and Oceania. The core of the collection was donated to the city by Baron Eduard von der Heydt in 1952. Highlights can be seen in the magnificent

neoclassical Villa Wesendonck, with ancient Oriental, Islamic and Indian painting and artefacts displayed in Villa Rieter. The Baldachine von Smaragd, a huge underground extension, opened in 2007.
ⓐ Gablerstr. 15 ☎ 044 206 31 31 ⓦ www.rietberg.ch 🕐 10.00–17.00 Tues–Sun (until 20.00 Wed), Apr–Sept; 10.00–17.00 Tues–Sun, Oct–Mar 🚊 Tram: 7 (Museum Rietberg). Admission charge

Uhrenmuseum Beyer Zurich (Clock & Watch Museum Beyer Zurich)

This small but fascinating museum in the basement of the celebrated Beyer Chronometrie store contains over 500 time-pieces ranging from wooden-wheel clocks, water clocks, sundials and traditional cuckoo-clocks to state-of-the-art contemporary navigational instruments. The shop sells many famous Swiss brands: Rolex, Cartier, Patek Philippe, Breitling, Jaeger LeCoultre...
ⓐ Bahnhofstr. 31 ☎ 043 344 63 63 ⓦ www.beyer-ch.com
🕐 14.00–18.00 Mon–Fri 🚊 Tram: 2, 6, 7, 8, 9, 11, 13 (Paradeplatz). Admission charge

Zunfthaus zur Meisen (Guildhall zur Meisen)

The Swiss National Museum's exhibition of porcelain and faience includes a fine collection of delicate 18th-century figurines and dishes from the Zurich porcelain factory in Kilchberg-Schooren. The Zunfthaus zur Meisen, one of the city's most beautiful guild houses, richly embellished with stuccos, is a perfect backdrop for the exquisite displays of baroque table decoration.
ⓐ Münsterhof 20 ☎ 044 221 28 07 ⓦ www.musee-suisse.com
🕐 10.30–17.00 Tues–Sun 🚊 Tram: 2, 6, 7, 8, 9, 11, 13 (Paradeplatz). Admission charge

RETAIL THERAPY

Alprausch A real souvenir alternative to Swiss chocolate, this young, trendy boutique epitomizes Swiss design with its urban fashions, snow-wear and accessories. ⓐ Werdmühlepl. 4 ⓣ 043 497 32 00 ⓦ www.alprausch.ch ⓛ 10.00–19.00 Mon–Fri, 10.00–17.00 Sat ⓝ Tram: 6, 7, 11, 13 (Bahnhofstrasse)

Amok One of Zurich's more unusual boutiques, specialising in skirts for men. ⓐ Ankerstr. 61 ⓣ 044 291 20 64 ⓦ www.amok.ch ⓛ 09.00–12.15, 13.00–18.30 Mon–Fri, 12.00–16.00 Sat ⓝ Tram: 2, 3 (Bezirksgebäude)

Bally Capitol The world's largest outlet of this famous Swiss institution. ⓐ Bahnhofstr. 66 ⓣ 044 224 39 39 ⓦ www.bally.ch ⓛ 09.30–19.00 Mon & Tues, 09.30–20.00 Wed–Fri, 09.30–17.00 Sat ⓝ Tram: 6, 7, 11, 13 (Bahnhofstrasse)

Bucherer An old favourite for jewellery and watches. Look out for Chopard, Tag Heuer, Rolex and other famous Swiss brands. ⓐ Bahnhofstr. 50 ⓣ 044 211 26 35 ⓦ www.bucherer.com ⓛ 09.00–19.00 Mon–Fri, 09.00–17.00 Sat ⓝ Tram: 6, 7, 11, 13 (Bahnhofstrasse)

Chäs Vreneli A small cheese shop, renowned beyond the Swiss borders for its selection of regional cheeses. Try the Tilsiter, Appenzeller, Emmental or, for fondue, some Gruyère and Vacherin Fribourgeois. ⓐ Münsterhof 7 ⓣ 044 221 32 81

🅦 www.chaes-vreneli.ch 🅛 06.30–18.30 Mon–Fri, 06.30–16.00
Sat 🅝 Tram: 2, 6, 7, 8, 9, 11, 13 (Paradeplatz)

Confiserie Sprüngli Sprüngli is Switzerland's most famous
chocolatier, founded in 1836. Still today the world-famous
pralinés, *truffes du jour*, *Luxembourgerli* (tiny, cream-filled,
coloured meringues) and other specialities are lovingly
handmade daily, following traditional recipes. Upstairs is
a coffee shop. 🅐 Bahnhofstr. 21, Am Paradepl. 🅣 044 224 47 11
🅦 www.spruengli.ch 🅛 07.30–18.30 Mon–Fri, 08.00–16.00 Sat
🅝 Tram: 2, 6, 7, 8, 9, 11, 13 (Paradeplatz)

Edo Popken In his small boutique at the heart of the banking
district, Swiss designer Edo Popken provides shirts and ties for
the best-dressed men in town. 🅐 Bärengasse 10 🅣 044 221 25 08
🅦 www.edopopken.ch 🅛 09.00–18.30 Mon–Fri (until 20.00 Thur),
09.00–17.00 Sat 🅝 Tram: 2, 6, 7, 8, 9, 11, 13 (Paradeplatz)

Fabric Frontline The exceptional silks here, ranging from ties
and scarves to reams of fabric in vivid colours and prints, draw
such designers as Lacroix, Givenchy and Vivienne Westwood
to this small textile house. 🅐 Ankerstr. 118 🅣 044 241 64 55
🅦 www.fabricfrontline.ch 🅛 10.00–18.30 Mon–Fri, 10.00–16.00
Sat 🅝 Tram: 8 (Helvetiaplatz)

Franz Carl Weber One of the largest toy shops in Europe
and every child's dream, with its impressive window displays
and dazzling range of toys for all ages. 🅐 Bahnhofstr. 62

⬤ *If you like meringue, you'll love* Luxembourgerli

☎ 044 225 78 78 ⓦ www.fcw.ch ⏰ 09.00–18.30 Mon–Fri (until 20.00 Thur), 09.00–17.00 Sat Ⓣ Tram: 6, 7, 11, 13 (Bahnhofstrasse)

Globus-City If you can't find it at Globus, you can probably do without it; there are seven floors of fashion, jewellery, toiletries, stationery, and a sensational delicatessen. ⓐ Schweizergasse 11 ☎ 044 226 60 60 ⓦ www.globus.ch ⏰ 09.00–20.00 Mon–Fri, 09.00–17.00 Sat Ⓣ Tram: 6, 7, 11, 13 (Bahnhofstrasse)

Grieder This spacious, sophisticated store specialises in prêt-a-porter, haute-couture and exclusive accessories for men and women by such designers as Armani, Kenzo, Gaultier, Fendi and Choo. ⓐ Bahnhofstr. 30 ☎ 044 224 36 36 ⓦ www.bongenie-grieder.ch ⏰ 09.00–18.30 Mon–Fri (until 20.00 Thur), 09.30–17.00 Sat Ⓣ Tram: 2, 6, 7, 8, 9, 11, 13 (Paradeplatz)

Jelmoli Zurich's largest and most popular department store. ⓐ Seidengasse 1 ☎ 044 220 44 11 ⓦ www.jelmoli.ch ⏰ 09.00–20.00 Mon–Fri, 09.00–17.00 Sat Ⓣ Tram: 6, 7, 11, 13 (Rennweg)

Pastorini Spielzeug A magical toy shop, with three floors of imaginative wooden toys, musical instruments, dolls and puppets, crafts and educational games. ⓐ Weinpl. 3 ☎ 044 228 70 70 ⓦ www.pastorini.ch ⏰ 13.30–18.30 Mon, 09.30–18.30 Tues–Fri, 09.30–17.00 Sat Ⓣ Tram: 6, 7, 11, 13 (Rennweg)

Schweizer Heimatwerk *The* shop for top-quality contemporary Swiss craftwork, with everything from ceramic kitchenware

and glass to jewellery and clothing, woodwork and toys.
Ⓐ Uraniastr. 1 Ⓣ 044 222 19 55 Ⓦ www.heimatwerk.ch
Ⓛ 09.00–20.00 Mon–Fri, 09.00–18.00 Sat Ⓝ Tram: 4, 15
(Rudolf-Brun-Brücke)

Sibler This wonderful design shop is brimming with witty yet
practical household items and gift ideas. Ⓐ Münsterhof 16
Ⓣ 044 211 55 50 Ⓦ www.sibler-shop.ch Ⓛ 10.00–19.00 Mon–Fri,
09.00–18.30 Sat Ⓝ Tram: 2, 6, 7, 8, 9, 11, 13 (Paradeplatz)

Spitzenhaus Labor An old-fashioned shop, filled with fine
table linens from Bern and Zurich and lace from St Gallen
and Appenzell. Ⓐ Börsenstr. 14 Ⓣ 044 211 55 76 Ⓛ 09.30–12.30,
13.30–18.30 Mon–Fri, 09.30–16.30 Sat Ⓝ Tram: 2, 8, 9, 11
(Bürkliplatz)

Swatch First launched in 1983, the simple, plastic Swiss-
designed Swatch is the most successful wrist-watch of
all time. Check out the latest seasonal collections here.
Ⓐ Bahnhofstr. 94 Ⓣ 044 221 28 66 Ⓦ www.swatch.ch
Ⓛ 09.30–19.00 Mon–Fri, 09.30–17.00 Sat Ⓝ Tram: 6, 7, 11, 13
(Bahnhofstrasse)

Teuscher This elaborately decorated Altstadt chocolate
shop tempts passers-by to stop for a box of speciality
handmade truffles. Try the champagne and orange ones!
Ⓐ Storchengasse 9 Ⓣ 044 211 51 53 Ⓦ www.teuscher.com
Ⓛ 08.00–18.30 Mon–Fri, 08.00–17.00 Sat, 16.00–18.00 Sun
Ⓝ Tram: 2, 6, 7, 8, 9, 11, 13 (Paradeplatz)

TAKING A BREAK

• **Confiserie Sprüngli £ ❶** The most select café in town, overlooking Paradeplatz, full of old-time Zürchers enjoying fine cakes, chocolates and *pâtisseries*. ⓐ Bahnhofstr. 21, Am Paradepl. ⓣ 044 224 47 31 ⓦ www.confiserie-spruengli.ch ⓛ 07.30–18.30 Mon–Fri, 08.00–17.00 Sat ⓝ Tram: 2, 6, 7, 8, 9, 11, 13 (Paradeplatz)

Mishio £–££ ❷ Trendy, minimalist noodle bar serving tasty pan-Asian cuisine to eat in or take away. ⓐ Sihlstr. 9 ⓣ 044 228 76 76 ⓦ www.mishio.ch ⓛ 06.30–23.00 Mon–Sat ⓝ Tram: 6, 7, 11, 13 (Rennweg)

Bona Dea ££ ❸ This vegetarian buffet restaurant beside the Hauptbahnhof offers a wide choice of delicious salads and Asian-influenced dishes. ⓐ Bahnhofpl. 15 ⓣ 044 217 15 15 ⓛ 11.30–18.30 ⓝ Tram: 3, 4, 6, 7, 10, 11, 13, 14 (Bahnhofplatz)

• **Grieder ££ ❹** A favourite haunt for well-heeled shoppers. Enjoy a coffee or a light lunch on the tree-shaded rooftop terrace. ⓐ Bahnhofstr. 30 ⓣ 044 224 36 36 ⓦ www.bongenie-grieder.ch ⓛ 09.00–18.30 Mon–Fri (until 20.00 Thur), 09.30–17.00 Sat ⓝ Tram: 2, 6, 7, 8, 9, 11, 13 (Paradeplatz)

Hiltl ££ ❺ Hiltl was Europe's first vegetarian eatery when it opened in 1898. Today it remains Zurich's top vegetarian restaurant with an excellent salad bar and superb curries, too. ⓐ Sihlstr. 28 ⓣ 044 227 70 00 ⓦ www.hiltl.ch ⓛ 06.00–00.00 ⓝ Tram: 2, 6, 7, 8, 9, 11, 13 (Paradeplatz)

AFTER DARK

RESTAURANTS

- **Bierhalle Kropf £ ⑥** The 'Kropf', as it is fondly called by locals, serves hearty portions of traditional Zurich cuisine and fine beers in a Bavarian-style beer hall. ⓐ In Gassen 16 ① 044 221 18 05 ① 11.30–23.30 Mon–Sat ⓝ Tram: 2, 6, 7, 8, 9, 11, 13 (Paradeplatz)

Reithalle £ ⑦ The former military riding school has been converted into a bar, restaurant, theatre and centre of performing arts. Enjoy a variety of tasty, international dishes inside the stables or in the spacious cobblestone courtyard. There's also dancing on Saturday nights from 23.45. ⓐ Theaterhaus Gessnerallee, Gessnerallee 8 ① 044 212 70 66 ⓦ www.restaurant-reithalle.ch ① 11.00–00.00 Mon–Fri, 18.00–00.00 Sat, 18.00–23.00 Sun ⓝ Tram: 3

Zeughauskeller £ ⑧ A converted 15th-century arsenal, now the city's top beer hall, serves traditional Swiss cuisine alongside steins of local beer. The metre-long sausage feeds four. ⓐ Bahnhofstr. 28A ① 044 211 26 90 ⓦ www.zeughauskeller.ch ① 11.30–23.00 ⓝ Tram: 2, 6, 7, 8, 9, 11, 13 (Paradeplatz)

Contrapunto ££ ⑨ Linger over a meal on the pavement terrace at this elegant modern Italian restaurant. ⓐ Waaggasse 5/7 ① 044 211 65 25 ① 11.30–23.30 ⓝ Tram: 2, 6, 7, 8, 9, 11, 13 (Paradeplatz)

Tao's ££–£££ ⑩ Join the beautiful people for delicious Euro-Asian cuisine in this sophisticated, modern-Oriental restaurant-cum-lounge bar and candlelit garden. ⓐ Augustinergasse 3

☎ 044 448 11 22 **🌐** www.taos-lounge.com **🕐** 12.00–01.00 Mon–Sat **🚋** Tram: 6, 7, 11, 13 (Rennweg)

Caduff's Wine Loft £££ ⓫ This stylish restaurant boasts more than 2,500 different wines, a tempting Mediterranean menu and the longest bar in town. **📍** Kanzleistr. 126 **☎** 044 240 22 55 **🌐** www.wineloft.ch **🕐** 11.30–14.00, 17.00–00.00 Mon–Fri, 17.00–00.00 Sat **🚋** Tram: 2, 3 (Kalkbreite); Tram: 8 (Bäckeranlage)

Seidenspinner £££ ⓬ This upmarket restaurant and beautiful garden terrace draws a media and fashion crowd. **📍** Ankerstr. 120 **☎** 044 241 07 00 **🌐** www.seidenspinner.ch **🕐** 12.00–15.00, 18.00–22.30 Tues–Fri, 18.00–22.30 Sat **🚋** Tram: 8 (Helvetiaplatz)

Zunfthaus zur Waag £££ ⓭ Top-notch Swiss cuisine in an exquisite setting within a beautiful 17th-century guildhouse. **📍** Münsterhof 8 **☎** 044 216 99 66 **🌐** www.zunfthaus-zur-waag.ch **🕐** 11.30–14.00, 18.00–22.00 **🚋** Tram: 2, 6, 7, 8, 9, 11, 13 (Paradeplatz)

BARS & CLUBS
Kaufleuten Rub shoulders with celebrities at one of the most glamorous nightclubs in town. **📍** Pelikanstr. 18 **☎** 044 225 33 22 **🌐** www.kaufleuten.com **🚋** Tram: 6, 7, 11, 13 (Rennweg)

Saint Germain New hotspot on top of the Bally building, overlooking Bahnhofstrasse. The restaurant has a touch of cosmopolitan class and the club is the hottest place for young and beautiful it-people. **📍** Bahnhofstrasse 66 **☎** 044 215 90 00 **🌐** www.saintgermain.ch **🚋** Tram: 6,7,11,13 (Rennweg)

Niederdorf & beyond

The picturesque Niederdorf district, on the right bank of the
Limmat river, forms the eastern half of the city's Altstadt and
provides a perfect counterpart to glitzy, glamorous Central
Zurich on the left bank, with its chic shopping streets and
finance houses. Niederdorf has a special, village-like charm with
its hilly, cobbled lanes, medieval houses painted in pastel shades
and historic guildhalls. Its centrepiece is the Grossmünster,
a veritable city landmark with its enormous twin towers. Above
the Altstadt is the university with its grandiose architecture,
and Switzerland's top gallery, the Kunsthaus. To the south there
is a wonderful lakeside walk to Zürichhorn Park, past lidos, boat
hire, cafés, museums and ornamental gardens.

SIGHTS & ATTRACTIONS

Botanischer Garten der Universität Zurich
(Botanic Garden of Zurich University)

The stunning plant collections here provide a botanical world
tour, from alpine roses and Mediterranean herbs to desert
plants and tropical rainforests. ⓐ Zollikerstr. 107 ⓣ 044 634 83 31
ⓦ www.bguz.unizh.ch ⓛ Garden: 08.00–18.00 Mon–Fri,
08.00–17.00 Sat & Sun; greenhouse: 09.30–16.00 ⓝ Bus: 33, 77
(Botanischer Garten)

Chinagarten Zurich (Zurich China Garden)

This lovely traditional South China garden was a gift from
Zurich's twin town, Kunming. Dedicated to 'the three winter

HEADLESS SAINTS!

Zurich's cathedral is dedicated to the city's patron saints, Felix, Regula and Exuperantius, who attempted to convert its citizens to Christianity in the 3rd century. According to legend, the governor of the city made them drink molten lead and plunged them into boiling oil. They still refused to renounce their faith, so they were beheaded. Miraculously, even this didn't stop them. They picked up their heads, carried them to the top of a hill (where the cathedral stands today), dug their own graves and then buried themselves. Zurich's seal still honours these martyrs, portrayed carrying their heads under their arms. Their remains are kept in one of the Grossmünster's chapels.

friends' (pine, bamboo and winter cherry), and with ponds, pagodas, exotic planting and inscriptions and paintings, it is an oasis of calm at Zürichhorn Park. ⓐ Bellerivestr. ⓣ 044 435 22 52/51 ⓦ www.chinagarten.ch ⓛ 11.00–19.00 mid-Mar–mid-Oct ⓝ Bus: 912, 916 (Chinagarten). Admission charge

Grossmünster (Cathedral)

This imposing Romanesque and Gothic cathedral with its two mighty towers stands proudly on a terrace overlooking the Limmat river. According to legend, it was founded by Charlemagne, whose horse faltered at the graves of three early Christian martyrs, Zurich's patron saints Felix and Regula, and their servant Exuperantius.

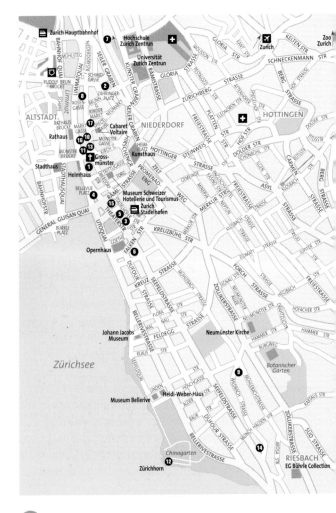

Niederdorf
& beyond

0   250 metres
0   250 yards

In the early 16th century, it was the parish church of Huldrych Zwingli and the birthplace of the Reformation (see page 16). In accordance with Zwingli's beliefs, the interior of the Grossmünster is austere. The choir contains striking red and blue stained-glass windows by Augusto Giacometti, which depict the Christmas story, and there is a Renaissance statue of Charlemagne in the crypt, a copy of which crowns the south tower. The bird's eye views from the top of the tower merit the 187-step climb.
ⓐ Grossmünsterpl. ☎ 044 252 59 49 ⓛ 09.00–18.00 mid-Mar–Oct; 10.00–17.00 Nov–mid-Mar ⓝ Tram: 4. Admission charge for tower

Niederdorf

The eastern part of Zurich's Altstadt is centred on the Niederdorf, a predominantly car-free, village-like district known to locals as the 'Dörfli', which stretches southwards along the riverside for about a kilometre. With its cobbled alleyways awash with small cafés, bars and boutiques, and its sunny courtyards splashed with medieval fountains, it is one of Zurich's most popular districts. During summer months on Niederdorfstrasse (the main street), the cafés and restaurants spill out onto pavement terraces to create a lively atmosphere. ⓝ Tram: 4, 15 (Rathaus or Helmhaus); Tram: 3, 4, 6, 7, 10, 15 (Central); Tram: 3 (Neumarkt)

Utoquai

Join sun-seekers at one of the most popular lakeside lidos, with its smart sun-terrace, bar, restaurant, sauna and massage facilities, and boat hire. ☎ 044 251 61 51 ⓛ 07.00–20.00 mid-May–mid-Sept ⓝ Tram: 2, 4 (Kreuzstrasse). Admission charge

Zoo Zurich

The city zoo is more than just an animal park. It focuses on endangered animals and attempts to provide authentic habitats for its more than 360 species of animals from around the globe. It has even recreated a Masoala rainforest in its midst. Young children love the Zoolino petting area. ⓐ Zürichbergstr. 221 ⓘ 044 254 25 05 ⓦ www.zoo.ch ⓒ 09.00–18.00 Mar–Oct (Masoala rainforest from 10.00); 09.00–17.00 Nov–Feb (Masoala rainforest from 10.00) ⓝ Tram: 5, 6 (Zoo). Admission charge

⬥ *A typical narrow, cobbled lane, Niederdorf*

Zürichsee (Lake Zurich)

One of the city's most pleasurable experiences is to stroll along the east bank of the lake, admire its beautiful scenery by day and by night, and enjoy its many facilities, which range from pedalo hire to steamboat excursions, restaurants, lidos, picnic areas, gardens and even an open-air cinema in summer. Look out for the **Johann Jacobs Museum**, dedicated to coffee (ⓐ Seefeldquai 17 ⓦ www.johann-jacobs-museum.ch. Admission charge); the attractive **Museum Bellerive**, with its changing exhibitions of applied arts (ⓐ Höschgasse 3 ⓦ www.museum-bellerive.ch. Admission charge); the Chinagarten; and Jean Tinguely's perpetual-motion sculpture *Heureka*, built for the 1964 National Exhibition. Take a break at one of the cafés or enjoy fresh fish at Fischstube Zürichhorn (see page 91) and, whatever you do, enjoy the tranquillity of the lake away from the frenetic city centre.

CULTURE

Cabaret Voltaire

The Dada art movement was founded here at Cabaret Voltaire almost a hundred years ago in 1916, and was a popular rendezvous for such artists and writers as Hans Arp and Hugo Ball (see page 14). Today it contains a small museum devoted to Dadaism and an arty upstairs café. ⓐ Spiegelgasse 1 ⓣ 043 268 57 20 ⓦ www.cabaretvoltaire.ch ⓛ Museum: 13.00–19.00 Tues–Sun; café: 11.30–19.00 Tues–Sun ⓝ Tram: 4, 15 (Rathaus). Admission charge

E G Bührle Collection

One of the world's most celebrated private art collections, housed in an elegant 19th-century villa. Industrialist Ernst Bührle's paintings include some major old master works, but the focal point is his dazzling French Impressionist collection, with significant works by such artists as Cézanne, Monet, Picasso, Renoir and Van Gogh. Since the big robbery here in early 2008 opening times have been temporarily restricted. Check the website for the latest info. ⓐ Zollikerstr. 172 ⓣ 044 422 00 86 ⓦ www.buehrle.ch ⓛ 14.00–17.00 Tues, Wed, Fri & Sun ⓝ Tram: 2, 4 (Wildbachstrasse). Admission charge

Heidi-Weber-Haus, Centre Le Corbusier

'A house is a machine for living in' once remarked the celebrated Swiss architect and visual artist Le Corbusier. He created the Heidi-Weber-Haus to represent the culmination of his studies in the fields of architecture, interior design and visual arts, and to serve as a museum of his life and works. The resulting minimalist edifice of glass and steel, with its brightly coloured enamel blocks and umbrella roof, was his last building, completed posthumously in 1967, and reflects his ideological formalism. ⓐ Höschgasse 8 ⓣ 044 383 64 70 ⓦ www.lecorbusier-center.com ⓛ 14.00–18.00 Sat & Sun ⓝ Bus: 912, 916 (Chinagarten). Admission charge

Helmhaus & Wasserkirche (Water Church)

According to legend, the gothic Water Church was constructed on the execution site of Felix and Regula, Zurich's patron saints (see page 79). As with the city's other churches, it was robbed of its treasures during the Reformation. The adjacent Baroque

Helmhaus has been used as a courtroom and a covered market over the years. Today it is an imaginative exhibition space for young artists to showcase contemporary Swiss art. ⓐ Limmatquai 31 ⓣ 044 251 61 77 ⓦ www.helmhaus.org ⓛ 10.00–18.00 Tues–Sun ⓝ Tram: 4, 15 (Helmhaus)

Kunsthaus (Museum of Fine Arts)

The collections in Switzerland's premier gallery span Swiss and International art from the Middle Ages to the present day, and contain major loans of Impressionist and Expressionist works. The museum counts among the most modern and sophisticated in Europe, and its audio-guides provide in-depth information on over 200 artworks by all the big names, including Rembrandt, Rubens, Tiepolo, Monet, Picasso, Rodin, Dalí, Lichtenstein and Pollock. Highlights include paintings by Zürcher Post-Reformation artists, 19th- and 20th-century Swiss art, the Edvard Munch collection (the largest outside Oslo), and the Swiss-born Alberto Giacometti Foundation. ⓐ Heimpl. 1 ⓣ 044 253 84 84 ⓦ www.kunsthaus.ch ⓛ 10.00–21.00 Tues–Thur, 10.00–17.00 Fri–Sun ⓝ Tram: 3, 5, 8, 9 (Kunsthaus). Admission charge

Museum Schweizer Hotellerie & Tourismus (Swiss Hostelry & Tourism Museum)

Trace Switzerland's world-famous hospitality and tourism history through temporary exhibitions in this tiny but fascinating townhouse museum in Niederdorf. ⓐ Trittligasse 8 ⓣ 044 391 82 78 ⓛ 14.00–17.00 Wed & Fri, 11.00–17.00 Sat, 11.00–13.00 Sun, May–Dec ⓝ Tram: 4, 15 (Helmhaus)

Universität (University)

Zurich boasts Switzerland's leading university, the Federal Institute of Technology (ETH), which, over the years, has produced 28 Nobel Prize winners, including Albert Einstein, who especially enjoyed the city views from the Polyterrace, which is open to visitors. The university complex contains several specialist museums, including the **Archäologische Sammlung der Universität** (Archaeological Collection ⓦ www.archinst.unizh.ch), the **Graphische Sammlung der ETH** (Collection of Prints and Drawings ⓦ www.gs.ethz.ch) and the **Zoologisches Museum der Universität** (ⓦ www.unizh.ch/zoolmus). ❸ Rämistr. 71 ❶ 044 635 44 01 ⓦ www.uzh.ch

🔺 *The Chinagarten Zurich is an oasis of calm*

RETAIL THERAPY

Andy Jllien Swiss-designed shoes for all occasions from sandals with teetering heels to multi-coloured loafers and jazzy Wellington boots. ⓐ Torgasse 5–6 ⓣ 044 252 19 11 ⓛ 11.00–18.30 Mon, 09.30–18.30 Tues–Fri (until 19.00 Thur), 09.30–17.00 Sat ⓝ Tram: 2, 4, 5, 8, 9, 11, 15 (Bellevue)

Neumarkt 17 One of the most extraordinary shops in Zurich, this is a rabbit warren of stylish interior design and modern furnishing. ⓐ Neumarkt 17 ⓣ 044 254 38 38 ⓦ www.neumarkt17.ch ⓛ 09.00–18.30 Tues–Fri, 09.00–17.00 Sat ⓝ Tram: 3 (Neumarkt)

🔺 *Schwarzenbach, an old-fashioned Niederdorf grocery shop*

* **Schwarzenbach** An old-fashioned grocery shop in Niederdorf specializing in 'colonial goods', including teas, coffee, nuts, dried fruit, herbs and spices, oils and chocolates. There is a small café, too. ⓐ Münstergasse 19 ⓣ 044 261 13 15 ⓦ www.schwarzenbach.ch ⓛ 08.00–18.30 Tues–Fri, 09.00–17.00 Sat ⓝ Tram: 4, 15 (Rathaus)

TAKING A BREAK

Altstadt £ ❶ This cool café-bar near the Grossmünster is a popular meeting point for breakfast, coffee, lunch or a relaxed aperitif. ⓐ Kirchgasse 4 ⓣ 044 250 53 53 ⓦ www.hotel-altstadt.ch ⓛ 07.00–00.00 ⓝ Tram: 4, 15 (Helmhaus)

Café Zähringer £ ❷ Popular with students, this bright, atmospheric café serves healthy, organic, mostly vegetarian food. ⓐ Zähringerpl. 11 ⓣ 044 252 05 00 ⓦ www.cafe-zaehringer.ch ⓛ 08.00–00.00 Tues–Sun ⓝ Tram: 4, 15 (Rudolf-Brun-Brücke)

Mövenpick Ice Cream Gallery £ ❸ Treat yourself to a Swiss-made ice-cream, by the lake, in a bewildering choice of flavours, including espresso, pistachio, grapefruit, apple, Swiss chocolate… ⓐ Theaterstr. 8 ⓣ 043 268 04 20 ⓦ www.moevenpick-icecream.com ⓛ 11.00–23.00 ⓝ Tram: 2, 4, 5, 8, 9, 11, 15 (Bellevue)

* **Sternen Grill £ ❹** This sausage stand serves the best fast food in town. Even local resident Tina Turner queues here for a 'St Galler Bratwurst mit Gold Burli' (a sausage wrapped in paper, a bowl of mustard to dunk it in, and a crusty roll).

ⓐ Bellevuepl. ⓣ 044 251 49 49 ⓛ 10.00–00.00 ⓝ Tram: 2, 4, 5, 8, 9, 11, 15 (Bellevue)

● **Globus-Bellevue ££** ❺ Eat your way around the world with light bites and takeaway tapas, panini, noodles, curries and sushi. ⓐ Theaterstr. 12 ⓣ 044 266 16 16 ⓦ www.globus.ch ⓛ 07.00–00.00 Mon–Sat, 10.00–22.00 Sun ⓝ Tram: 2, 4, 5, 8, 9, 11, 15 (Bellevue)

Tibits by Hiltl ££ ❻ Vegetarian fast food for fashionable, health-conscious Zürchers. Try the sensational buffet. ⓐ Seefeldstr. 2 ⓣ 044 260 32 22 ⓦ www.tibits.ch ⓛ 06.30–00.00 Mon–Fri, 08.00–00.00 Sat, 09.00–00.00 Sun ⓝ Tram: 2, 4 (Opernhaus)

AFTER DARK

RESTAURANTS

Crazy Cow £ ❼ Hearty Swiss cuisine in a witty restaurant decorated with cartoons, cows, Heidi, Toblerone and other kitsch local memorabilia. Even the menu is in Swiss dialect (with English translations). Try the scrumptuous *rösti* dishes or the Alpen Macaroni. ⓐ Leonhardstr. 1 ⓣ 044 261 40 55 ⓦ www.crazycow.ch ⓛ 11.00–23.00 ⓝ Tram: 6, 7, 10, 15 (Haldenegg)

● **Adler's Swiss Chuchi £–££** ❽ Excellent-value fondues and *raclette* dishes in a bright, modern, alpine setting, plus plenty of authentic Swiss specialities for non-cheese-lovers, all washed down with local wines. At the end of the meal, the bill is presented inside a musical box. ⓐ Rosengasse 10

① 044 266 96 96 **⑩** www.hotel-adler.ch **🕐** 11.30–23.15
🚊 Tram: 4, 15 (Rudolf-Brun-Brücke)

Blinde Kuh £–££ ❾ As the world's first 'dark restaurant', the hugely popular Blinde Kuh ('Blind Man's Bluff') offers the unique experience of losing your sight for the duration of your meal as you dine in total darkness. No lights are allowed inside; you have to place your watch and mobile phone in a locker before you go in, to ensure total darkness, and even the waiters are blind or partially sighted. **ⓐ** Mühlebachstr. 148 **①** 044 421 50 50 **⑩** www.blindekuh.ch **🕐** 18.30–23.00 Tues–Sat, 18.00–23.00 Sun **🚊** Tram: 2, 4 (Höschgasse)

Bodega Espanola ££ ❿ This cosy, rustic, first-floor restaurant serves traditional Spanish fare. On the ground floor is a buzzing tapas bar. **ⓐ** Münstergasse 15 **①** 044 251 23 10 **🕐** Restaurant: 12.00–14.00, 18.00–00.00; tapas bar: 10.00–00.00 **🚊** Tram: 4, 15 (Rathaus)

Le Dezaley ££ ⓫ A friendly restaurant specialising in traditional Vaudois dishes, including superb fondues, served in a series of characterful, interconnecting dining rooms and a small courtyard garden in summer. **ⓐ** Römergasse 7, off Limmatquai **①** 044 251 61 29 **⑩** www.le-dezaley.ch **🕐** 11.30–14.00, 18.00–00.00 Mon–Sat **🚊** Tram: 4, 15 (Helmhaus)

Fischstube Zürichhorn ££ ⓬ One of the top fish restaurants, with a beautiful terrace beside the lake. **ⓐ** Bellerivestr. 160 **①** 044 422 25 20 **⑩** www.fischstube.ch **🕐** 09.30–23.30 May–Sept **🚊** Tram: 2, 4 (Opernhaus)

Mère Catherine ££ Enjoy Provençal cuisine at this small courtyard restaurant at the heart of Niederdorf. ⓐ Nägelihof 3, off Limmatquai ⓣ 044 250 59 40 ⓦ www.commercio.ch ⓛ 11.30–00.00 ⓝ Tram: 4, 15 (Rathaus)

Blaue Ente £££ Join Zurich's smart set for light and sophisticated French cooking in a converted ancient water mill on the banks of the lake, which combines old steam machines and giant water wheels with minimalist glass-and-chrome decor. At night the restaurant's lounge converts into a fashionable chill-out bar. ⓐ Seefeldstr. 223 ⓣ 044 388 68 40 ⓦ www.blaue-ente.ch ⓛ 11.30–00.30 Mon–Sat, 11.30–23.00 Sun ⓝ Tram: 2, 4 (Wildbachstrasse)

Kronenhalle £££ Join Zurich's movers and shakers in the city's top restaurant and enjoy upmarket Swiss staples in a traditional, rustic setting, with chandeliers and wood-panelled walls adorned with original canvases by such luminaries as Picasso, Chagall, Kandinsky and Matisse. ⓐ Rämistr. 4, off Limmatquai ⓣ 044 262 99 00 ⓦ www.kronenhalle.com ⓛ 12.00–00.00 ⓝ Tram: 2, 4, 5, 8, 9, 11, 15 (Bellevue)

Zunfthaus zum Rüden £££ Rich, hearty, Swiss cuisine in a stunning Gothic riverside guildhall. ⓐ Limmatquai 42 ⓣ 044 261 95 66 ⓦ www.hauszumrueden.ch ⓛ 12.00–15.00, 18.30–00.00 Mon–Fri ⓝ Tram: 4, 15 (Rathaus)

Zunfthaus zur Schmiden £££ The 16th-century 'Guildhall of the Smiths' provides a classy setting for fine Swiss-German

specialities. Try the delicious *Zürcher Geschnetzeltes*. ⓐ Marktgasse 20
ⓣ 044 250 58 48 ⓦ www.zunfthausschmiden.ch ⓛ 11.30–14.30,
18.00–23.30 Tues–Fri ⓝ Tram: 4, 15 (Rathaus)

BARS & CLUBS

Ba Ba Lu This trendy post-modern bar in Niederdorf, complete with
DJ and live music, attracts a young, lively crowd. ⓐ Schmidgasse 6
ⓣ 044 251 97 32 ⓝ Tram: 4, 15 (Rudolf-Brun-Brücke)

Mascotte One of the oldest clubs in Switzerland, situated in
a century-old bulding on the Bellevue. Host to artists such as
Josephine Baker and Louis Armstrong decades ago, nowadays
you can watch trendy rock and pop bands live. Parties range
from hiphop to rock. ⓐ Theaterstr. 10 ⓣ 044 260 15 80
ⓦ www.mascotte.ch

Zurich West

The city's former industrial quarter has undergone radical change in the past decade, most noticeably in the once-seedy 'Kreis 5' district around the site of the former Löwenbräu Brewery. It is now the heart of the city's hip scene, a multi-cultural area brimming with trendy bars, restaurants and clubs, and around-the-clock activity. The area is also notable for its inspirational architectural projects, with several old factories converted into living, office and leisure spaces. Shops, galleries and museums – including the Migros Museum and the Zurich Design Museum – focus on the latest trends in contemporary art, while the more traditional Swiss National Museum is among the nation's top museums.

SIGHTS & ATTRACTIONS

Flussbad Obere Letten

One of the trendiest and most popular lidos, where people come for a dip in the canal or a drift downstream in the river, past sundecks, *boules* and beach volleyball pitches. By night, the right bank of the canal turns into Pier West, an open-air bar with live DJs playing groovy sounds. ⓐ Lettensteg 10 ⓣ 044 362 92 00 ⓛ 09.00–20.00 mid-May–mid-Sept ⓝ Tram: 4, 13 (Limmatplatz)

Platzspitz

During the 1980s this spacious park behind the Swiss National Museum was sadly known as 'Needle Park', the largest meeting place for drug addicts in Switzerland, and best avoided by city dwellers. In 1993, the area was smartened up and it is now a popular and tranquil retreat stretching along the rivers Limmat and Sihl. It also marks the starting point for river cruises to the lake. ⓝ Tram: 4, 11, 13, 14 (Bahnhofquai)

Puls 5

Puls 5 is a trendy new lifestyle complex at the heart of the former industrial district of Zurich West, beside the Schiffbau. This architecturally innovative development contains at its heart a concrete-wrapped former Giessereihalle (foundry), together with a supermarket, fitness centre, apartments, shops, bars and restaurants. Still in its infancy, Puls 5 is fast becoming

◔ *Schweizerisches Landesmuseum is a Swiss cultural landmark*

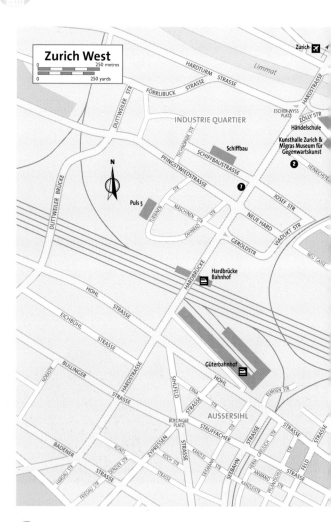

Zurich West

0 ——— 250 metres
0 ——— 250 yards

Zurich ✈

Limmat

HARDTURM STRASSE

FÖRRLIBUCK STRASSE

HARDSTRASSE

DUTTWEILER STR

TECHNOPARK STR

INDUSTRIE QUARTIER

ESCHER-WYSS PLATZ

ZÖLLY STR

Händelschule

SCHIFFBAUSTRASSE

Schiffbau

Kunsthalle Zurich & Migras Museum für Gegenwartskunst

❷

HENRICHSTR.

PFINGSTWIEDSTRASSE

N

DUTTWEILER BRÜCKE

Puls 5

TURBINEN STR

MASCHINEN STR

ZAHNRAD

STR

❶

JOSEF STR

NEUE HARD

VIADUKT STR

GEROLDSTR

NEU CASSE

HOHL STRASSE

HARDBRÜCKE

Hardbrücke Bahnhof

EICHBÜHL STRASSE

BULLINGER

HARDSTRASSE

Güterbahnhof

HOHL

REMSEN STR

NORDSTR

STRASSE

SIHLFELD STRASSE

ERNA STR

BADENER

BULLINGER PLATZ

AUSSERSIHL

STAUFFACHER

STR

STRASSE

STRASSE

ACNES

ZYPRESSEN

KANZELE

SEEBAHN

HERM

GREULICH STR

STR

FELD

STRASSE

HARDAU STR

DENZLER STR

KOCH STR

STRASSE

EBERMANN STR

ANWAND STR

KANZLEISTR

REGENSDORF

STR

FRIEDAU STR

SYBAHN STRASSE

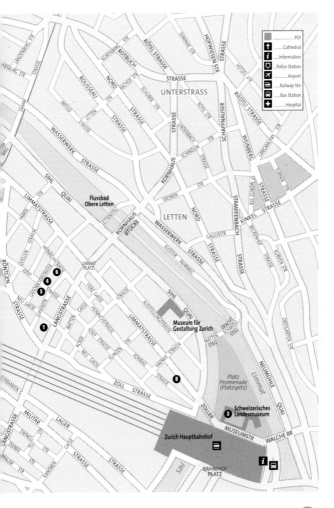

POI

- ▓ ......POI
- ✝ ......Cathedral
- ℹ ......Information
- ⊘ ......Police Station
- ✈ ......Airport
- 🚆 ......Railway Stn
- 🚌 ......Bus Station
- ✚ ......Hospital

UNTERSTRASS

LETTEN

Flussbad
Obere Letten

Museum für
Gestaltung Zurich

Platz
Promenade
(Platzspitz)

Schweizerisches
Landesmuseum

Zurich Hauptbahnhof

BAHNHOF
PLATZ

one of the hip addresses in town. Watch this space! ⓐ Puls 5, Turbinenpl. Ⓝ Tram: 4, 13 (Escher-Wyss-Platz)

Schiffbau

This striking 19th-century industrial building was once used for building ships and lake-cruisers. Today the ramshackle red-brick factory forms the heart of an avant-garde arts complex, containing a top-notch restaurant, bar, jazz club and a second stage for Zurich's best-known theatre, the Schauspielhaus. ⓐ Schiffbaustr. 4 (off Hardstr.) Ⓝ Tram: 4, 13 (Escher-Wyss-Platz)

CULTURE

Kunsthalle Zurich

One of two major museums in the converted Löwenbräu Brewery, the Kunsthalle focuses on the city's contemporary art scene with frequently changing exhibitions to showcase the work of up-and-coming internationally significant new artists. ⓐ Limmatstr. 270 (second floor) ⓣ 044 272 15 15 ⓦ www.kunsthallezurich.ch ⓛ 12.00–18.00 Tues, Wed & Fri, 12.00–20.00 Thur, 11.00–17.00 Sat & Sun Ⓝ Tram: 4, 13 (Dammweg). Admission charge (free Thur 17.00-20.00)

Migros Museum für Gegenwartskunst (Migros Museum for Contemporary Art)

The bright, lofty white rooms on the first floor of the former Löwenbräu Brewery building provide the perfect setting for modern art displays. The permanent collection contains around 1,300 artworks by 700 international artists, which rotate alongside temporary exhibitions. Make sure you also visit the world-class art galleries (for instance Hauser & Wirth) also located in the brewery buildings. ⓐ Limmatstr. 270 ⓣ 044 277 20 50 ⓦ www.migrosmuseum.ch ⓛ 12.00–18.00 Tues, Wed & Fri, 12.00–20.00 Thur, 11.00–17.00 Sat & Sun ⓝ Tram: 4, 13 (Dammweg). Admission charge

Museum für Gestaltung Zurich (Zurich Design Museum)

This top-notch museum features changing exhibitions on various aspects of design, architecture, photography, visual communications and multimedia, covering everything from 'Swiss-made' consumer goods to 'Gay Chic' and 'Take-away' (designs for eating on the move). The Plakatraum (Poster Collection) across the road within **Zurich's Design School** (ⓐ Limmatstr. 55) draws on an extensive archive of vintage posters for its temporary exhibitions. ⓐ Ausstellungsstr. 60 ⓣ 043 446 67 67 ⓦ www.museum-gestaltung.ch ⓛ 10.00–20.00 Tues–Thur, 10.00–17.00 Fri–Sun ⓝ Tram: 4, 13 (Museum für Gestaltung). Admission charge

Schweizerisches Landesmuseum (Swiss National Museum)

One of Zurich's top museums, it contains the world's largest collection of Swiss historical and cultural artefacts. It documents Swiss civilisation from pre-history to the modern age in over 100 rooms, with special emphasis on pre-history and the Middle Ages. Highlights include children's toys, silverware, Renaissance globes, regional costumes and an impressive collection of artefacts from each of the country's cantons. ⓐ Museumsstr. 2 ⓣ 044 218 65 11 ⓦ www.musee-suisse.ch ⓛ 10.00–17.00 Tues–Sun (till 21.00 Thur) ⓝ Tram: 4, 11, 13, 14 (Bahnhofquai). Admission charge

RETAIL THERAPY

Freitag Shop Zurich Surely the most unusual shop in town, the Freitag tower is a veritable mini-skyscraper, built out of 17 freight containers. It houses over 1,600 individually designed bags, wallets and accessories in all colours, shapes and sizes. ⓐ Geroldstr. 17 ⓣ 043 366 95 20 ⓦ www.freitag.ch ⓛ 11.00–19.30 Mon–Fri, 11.00–17.00 Sat ⓝ S-Bahn: Hardbrücke; Bus: 72, 33 (Pfingstweidstrasse)

🔺 *Freitag Shop Zurich, home of recycled chic*

TAKING A BREAK

Lily's Stomach Supply £ ❶ A trendy noodle bar serving delicious pan-Asian cuisine at long, communal tables. Ideal for those on a budget. Try the Pakistani curry or the Japanese *yaki soba* noodles, washed down with beers from around the world. ⓐ Langstr. 197 ❶ 044 440 18 85 ⓦ www.lilys.ch ❶ 11.00–00.00 Mon–Thur, 11.00–01.00 Fri & Sat, 15.00–00.00 Sun ⓝ Tram: 4, 13 (Limmatplatz)

Steinfels Restaurant £ ❷ Young, trendy restaurant with delightful, 70s-feel interior design and international cuisine. The beer is courtesy of their own brewery. ⓐ Heinrichstr. 267 ❶ 044 271 10 30 ⓦ www.steinfels-zuerich.ch ❶ 11.00-02.00 Fri & Sat, 11.00-23.00 Sun ⓝ Tram: 4,13 (Escher-Wyss-Platz)

Swiss Museum Café £ ❸ Enjoy coffee and cake or a light lunch snack at this jazzy, minimalist café in the Landesmuseum. ⓐ Museumsstr. 2 ❶ 044 218 65 11 ❶ 10.00–17.00 Tues–Sun ⓝ Tram: 4, 11, 13, 14 (Bahnhofquai)

AFTER DARK

RESTAURANTS
Al Posito Solito £ ❹ This old-fashioned, family-run Italian restaurant serves some of the best pizzas in town. ⓐ Gasometerstr. 26 ❶ 044 272 62 92 ❶ 11.30–14.00, 17.30–00.00 Mon–Fri, 18.00–00.00 Sat ⓝ Tram: 4, 13 (Limmatplatz)

Josef ££ ❺ Join the local 'in' crowd at this small but popular restaurant, with its stylish interior, exellent wine list and simple, Swiss-Italian menu. ⓐ Gasometerstr. 24 ❶ 044 271 65 95 Ⓦ www.josef.ch ❶ 11.30–14.00, 18.30–23.00 Mon–Fri, 18.30–23.00 Sat & Sun Ⓝ Tram: 4, 13 (Limmatplatz)

El Parador ££ ❻ Try the delicious prawns in garlic, paella or a variety of other authentic specialities in this highly regarded Spanish restaurant. ⓐ Luisenstr. 43 (cnr Heinrichstr.) ❶ 043 366 88 85 Ⓦ www.elparador.ch ❶ 11.30–14.30, 18.00–00.00 Mon–Fri Ⓝ Tram: 4, 13 (Limmatplatz)

LaSalle £££ ❼ The unusual setting and artful modern European cuisine draws Zurich's chic set to this sophisticated, minimalist restaurant. ⓐ Schiffbaustr. 4 ❶ 044 258 70 71 Ⓦ www.lasalle-restaurant.ch ❶ 11.00–00.00 Mon & Tues, 11.00–01.00 Wed & Thur, 11.00–02.00 Fri, 17.00–02.00 Sat, 17.00–00.00 Sun Ⓝ Tram: 4, 13 (Limmatplatz)

Sala of Tokyo £££ ❽ One of Switzerland's best Japanese restaurants. Booking essential. ⓐ Limmatstr. 29 ❶ 044 271 52 90 Ⓦ www.sala-of-tokyo.ch ❶ 11.45–14.00, 18.00–22.45 Tues–Fri, 18.00–22.45 Sat Ⓝ Tram: 4, 11, 13, 14 (Bahnhofquai)

BARS & CLUBS

Most of the district's nightlife is focused on trendy Limmatstrasse, with a cluster of bars and clubs around Escher-Wyss Platz too.

❶ *Elaborate window detail, Lucerne*

Lake Zurich (Zürichsee)

Lake Zurich offers an enormous choice of short excursions. Near the city, its shores are dominated by grassy parks, lakeside promenades and early 20th-century mansions. Further afield, picturesque villages such as Rapperswil and Küsnacht punctuate the shoreline, flanked by lush, green countryside and gentle hills – a veritable walker's paradise. Even the lake itself offers a wide variety of activities, including sailing, pleasure-boat cruising and swimming.

GETTING AROUND

The region is easy to explore by boat, on foot or on wheels.

By boat

The options are many: a day cruise to Rapperswil for lunch, museums and shopping; a morning cruise from Thalwil to Küsnacht for a lazy lakeside lunch; or escape the crowds and enjoy a relaxing stroll on the island of Ufenau. The **Zürichsee Schifffahrtsgesellschaft** (ⓐ Mythenquai 333 ❶ 044 487 13 33 ⓦ www.zsg.ch) offers a variety of excursions from two-hour mini-cruises to full day outings. During summer months ZSG ferries stop at every lakeside town.

By bike

The lake region is also ideal for cyclists. You can either pedal round the lake (along the 'Seestrasse'), or ride a section of National Bike Route Number 9; called the 'Route des Lacs', this is one of

nine national bicycle touring routes, and it takes keen cyclists right across Switzerland from Lake Constance to Lake Geneva. Bikes are available for rental at train stations in Rapperswil, Uznach, Ziegelbrücke, Forch and the Zurich Hauptbahnhof.
🕿 0900 300 300 Ⓦ www.rentabike.ch

By S-Bahn

The train lines run the length of both shores, offering an easy, scenic journey to such destinations as Rapperswil and Küsnacht. Depending on the time you wish to travel, you may consider purchasing a 9-Uhr Tagespass (9 o'clock Daypass), valid after 09.00 Monday to Friday and all day Saturday and Sunday.

🔺 *Sailing on the Zürichsee*

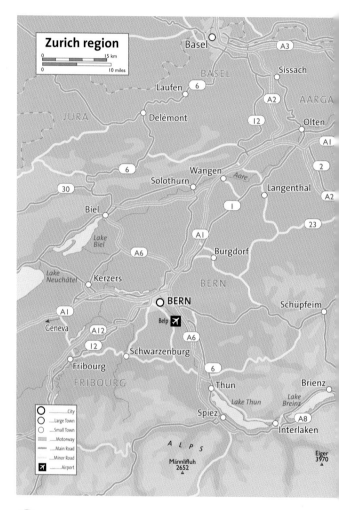

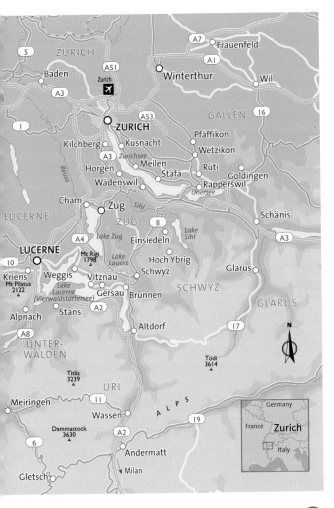

SIGHTS & ATTRACTIONS

Alpamare
Europe's largest indoor water-park, with ten thrilling water-slides, fun indoor and outdoor pools and wellness attractions too, including Switzerland's only iodine brine pool, thermal pools, whirlpools and saunas. ⓐ Gwattstr. 12, Pfäffikon ⓣ 055 415 15 15 ⓦ www.alpamare.ch ⓛ 10.00–22.00 Tues–Thur, 10.00–23.00 Fri, 09.00–23.00 Sat, 09.00–22.00 Sun & Mon ⓝ S-Bahn: S2, S8 (Pfäffikon). Admission charge

Knies Kinderzoo (Knies Children's Zoo)
Children adore this well-known children's zoo, where they can pet, stroke and feed many of the 300-plus animals here, marvel at the performing sea lions, and ride elephants, camels and ponies. ⓐ Oberseestr. 41, Rapperswil ⓣ 055 220 67 60 ⓦ www.knieskinderzoo.ch ⓛ 09.00–18.00 Mon–Sun ⓝ S-Bahn: S5, S7 (Rapperswil). Admission charge

Küsnacht
The hamlet of Küsnacht basks on the Goldküste ('Gold Coast'), the fashionable, eastern side of the lake, named after its golden afternoon sunshine and glorious sunsets. Since 1986 it has been home to American pop star, Tina Turner. The main appeal of Küsnacht is its celebrated restaurant. It also marks the start of the Küsnachter Tobel, a beautiful 7-km (4½-mile) pathway through shady forest, with excellent lake vistas en route. The lido is popular during summer months. ⓝ S-Bahn: S6, S7, S16

Rapperswil

This atmospheric lakeside town is sometimes called the 'City of Roses', due to its numerous rose gardens. One of the most delightful gardens is designed for the blind, with highly fragranced specimens and information in brail. Another lies within the 16th-century Cappuchin monastery. Other highlights include the Knies Children's Zoo (see page 108), the Circus Museum and an impressive medieval castle that contains a small museum devoted to Switzerland's Polish community (ⓦ www.muzeum-polskie.org ⏰ 13.00–17.00 Apr–Oct). Explore the narrow streets and alleys of the medieval old town and be sure to pause a while in Fischmarktplatz, the most picturesque square – open to the lake and fringed with café terraces and a small marina. ➌ Rapperswil Zürichsee Tourismus, Fischmarktpl. 1 ❶ 0848 811 500 ⏰ 10.00–17.00 Apr–Oct; 13.00–17.00 Nov–Mar ⓝ Hourly boat from Bürklipl. (duration two hours); S-Bahn: S5, S7 (Rapperswil)

Stäfa

The main attraction of this unremarkable town is that it is the lake's largest wine-producing community, located at the foot of the Pfannenstiel (pan handle) – the main vine-growing area of the canton – near the stunning 27.6-km (17-mile) **Pfannenstiel Panoramaweg** (panoramic footpath ⓦ www.zpp.ch). Two wine paths also start in Stäfa, with information panels providing wine lovers with valuable facts and figures about the grapes and wine culture of the lake. ⓝ S-Bahn: S7

Ufenau

Escape the city hubbub and visit the tranquil island of Ufenau during your lake cruise. The largest of two islands in the lake and measuring just 750 m by 200 m (2,460 ft by 656 ft), it is a perfect place to relax and enjoy nature. Stroll round the

◓ *Lake Zurich's 'Gold Coast'*

perimeter, sunbathe, visit the St Peter and St Paul Church with its second-century Gallo-Romanic temple, or enjoy a meal at the self-service restaurant (🕒 Mar–Oct). Regrettably, swimming on the island is prohibited as it is a protected nature reserve. ⓦ www.ufenau.ch Ⓝ Boat (see ⓦ www.zsg.ch)

Wädenswil

Winter is the best time to visit Wädenswil, when the natural outdoor ice skating rink beside the lake is open. ① 043 477 91 51 ⓦ www.eisbahnwaedi.ch 🕒 Check the website for rink's opening times Ⓝ S-Bahn: S2, S8 (Wädenswil). Admission charge

CULTURE

Bergwerkmuseum Käpfnach (Coal Mining Museum)

Housed within an 18th-century coal storeroom, this unusual museum provides a rare glimpse into the history of coal mining and especially the miners' day-to-day lifestyle. ⓐ Bergwerkstr. 27, Horgen ① 044 725 39 35 ⓦ www.horgen.net 🕒 13.00–16.30 Sat, Apr–Nov Ⓝ S-Bahn: S2, S8. Admission charge

Circus Museum Rapperswil

A fascinating insight into the history of Rapperswil's famous Knie family and its National Circus, its animal training and circus stunts, through colourful exhibits of ancient costumes, old posters, rare props and video films. Children especially enjoy trying on the old costumes in the 'kids' corner'. ⓐ Fischmarktpl. 1, Rapperswil ① 055 220 57 57 🕒 10.00–17.00 Apr–Oct; 13.00–17.00 Nov–Mar Ⓝ S-Bahn: S5, S7 (Rapperswil). Admission charge

FURTHER AFIELD

Atzmännig

A trip to Atzmännig makes a fun day out as it is home to Switzerland's most exciting summer toboggan run. At 700 m (2,297 ft) long, its sharp bends, steep gradients and tunnels provide an adrenaline rush for all the family. During summer months there are wonderful country walks. In winter, the snowy slopes are popular with skiers and snowboarders. ⓐ Sportbahnen Atzmännig, Goldingen ⓣ 055 284 64 34 ⓦ www.atzmaennig.ch ⓛ 10.00–11.45, 13.15–17.00 Mon–Fri, 08.30–17.15 Sat & Sun, Apr–May; 08.30-17.15 Sat & Sun, June–Sept; 08.30–11.45, 13.15–17.00 Mon–Fri, Oct; 09.00–17.00 Sat & Sun, mid-Nov–Mar ⓝ Train: Atzmännig

Einsiedeln

Set in picture-postcard scenery less than an hour by train south of Lake Zurich, the town of Einsiedeln is the nation's most important pilgrimage site, drawing a quarter of a million devotees annually to its vast Kloster, the Baroque Benedictine Abbey. Its lavish interior contains a much-revered Black Madonna, and there are daily guided tours, which provide a fascinating insight into the life of the monks and the history of the abbey.
Einsiedeln Tourismus ⓐ Hauptstr. 85, Einsiedeln ⓣ 055 418 44 88 ⓦ ww.einsiedeln.ch ⓛ 08.30–17.00 Mon–Fri, 09.00–16.00 Sat, 10.00–13.00 Sun, Apr–Nov; 08.30–17.00 Mon–Fri, 09.00–16.00 Sat, 09.00–12.00 Sun, Dec–Mar
Kloster Einsiedeln ⓐ Benzigerstr., Einsiedeln ⓣ 055 418 61 11 ⓦ www.kloster-einsiedeln.ch ⓛ 05.30–20.30 ⓝ Train: Einsiedeln (change at Wädenswil)

Hoch Ybrig

Zurich's nearest ski resort is easily accessible by train. In summer, hikers enjoy the idyllic landscape in the foothills of the Alps. In winter, it becomes a winter sports paradise, offering both downhill and cross-country skiing. The children's ski school is one of the best in Switzerland.

Ferien & Sportzentrum Hoch Ybrig ⓐ Waagtalstr. 127, Hoch Ybrig ⓣ 055 414 60 60 ⓦ www.hoch-ybrig.ch or www.ybrig.ch ⓝ Train: to Einsiedeln, then bus

TAKING A BREAK

Marsala ££ A smart, modern restaurant serving tasty Italian and Sicilian dishes near the harbour. ⓐ Seequai/Marktgasse 21, Rapperswil ⓣ 055 211 22 24 ⓦ www.marsala.ch ⓛ 11.00–14.00, 18.00–00.00 Mon–Fri, 11.00–00.00 Sat & Sun

Schützenhaus ££ A small, popular fish restaurant with beautiful views and alfresco dining, right on the lake. ⓐ Seestr. 48, Stäfa ⓣ 044 926 13 58 ⓛ 10.00–00.00 Thur–Mon

AFTER DARK

RESTAURANTS

Petermann's Kunststuben £££ Reputedly the best restaurant in Switzerland. Michelin-starred Horst Petermann's inventive cuisine is served with elegance and artistic flair in an intimate dining room. ⓐ Seestr. 160, Küsnacht ⓣ 044 910 07 15

ⓦ www.kunststuben.com ⓒ 12.00–14.00, 19.00–21.00
Tues–Sat ⓢ S-Bahn: S6, S7, S16 (Küsnacht)

Schloss Rapperswil £££ Rapperswil's top restaurant, located
within the castle, and best-known for its sensational fish and
seafood dishes. ⓣ 055 210 18 28 ⓦ www.schloss-restaurant.ch
ⓒ 11.30–23.30 Tues–Sat, 11.30–15.00 Sun

⬤ *Zürchers flock to the lake at weekends*

ACCOMMODATION

Camping Lützelau £ An idyllic campsite on the tiny island of
Lützelau with barbecue and picnic areas, and a small restaurant.
ⓐ Lützelau ⓣ 055 410 34 52 ⓦ www.luetzelau.ch ⓛ May–Sept
Ⓝ Island taxi boat (ⓣ 076 226 27 28): from Rapperswil

Jakob £ A popular choice at the heart of the old town, with
20 simple but stylish rooms, a classic bistro, trendy bar and
beautiful vaulted wine cellar. ⓐ Hauptpl. 11, Rapperswil
ⓣ 055 220 00 50 ⓦ www.jakob-hotel.ch

Hirschen-am-See ££ A friendly, country-style guesthouse on the
lake, in the small village of Meilen, with two restaurants and
panoramic views. ⓐ Seestr. 856, Meilen ⓣ 044 925 05 00
ⓦ www.hirschen-meilen.ch

Sonne ££ A romantic hotel in a beautiful location on the shore
of the lake, with fine dining, fine art (paintings and sculptures
by such artists as Tinguely and Warhol) and its very own beer
garden and pier. ⓐ Seestr. 120, Küsnacht ⓣ 044 914 18 18
ⓦ www.sonne.ch

Lucerne (Luzern)

The city of Lucerne (Luzern in German) is every bit as picturesque as the postcards promise. With its remarkable blend of lakes, mountains, history, culture, folklore and architecture, this charming medieval town in central Switzerland has it all. Little wonder it is a tourist magnet.

Lucerne is located on the northern edge of Lake Lucerne (Vierwaldstättersee) at the foot of majestic Mount Pilatus, and is surrounded by spectacular alpine scenery steeped in

● *The iconic Kapellbrücke*

the history of William Tell and the formation of the Swiss Confederation. The old quarter of town is located on the edge of the lake, and brims with charm and character. Its picturesque streets are dotted with historical monuments, fortifications and churches. The spacious riverbank promenades are ideal for strolling, and the breathtaking countryside is celebrated for its walks, panoramas, folklore and sports.

GETTING THERE

It takes just 50 minutes to reach Lucerne by train from the Zurich Hauptbahnhof (with departures every half hour). For further details of transport, sightseeing or accommodation, contact the tourist office:
Luzern Tourismus ⓐ Bahnhofstr. 3 ⓣ 041 227 17 17
ⓦ www.luzern.org

SIGHTS & ATTRACTIONS

Kapellbrücke (Chapel Bridge)
Europe's oldest covered wooden footbridge, spanning the Reuss river, is very much a symbol of Lucerne and the most photographed monument in Switzerland. Following a fire in 1993, it has undergone a major restoration project, including the reproduction of many of its remarkable Renaissance wall paintings.

Löwendenkmal (Lion Monument)
This world-famous monument – 'the dying Lion of Lucerne' – was carved into the sandstone cliff above the town in 1821 to

commemorate the heroic deaths of Swiss mercenaries who died in Paris in 1792 trying to save the life of Marie Antoinette. Mark Twain described it as 'the saddest and most moving piece of rock in the world'. ⓐ Denkmalstr. 4

Mt Pilatus

The ascent of Mt Pilatus (2,132 m/6,993 ft), the giant, mystic mountain looming over Lucerne, is one of the most popular excursions in Switzerland. Until the 17th century, people were forbidden to climb it because locals feared that Pontius Pilate's ghost would bring about the downfall of Lucerne. According to legend, his body was brought here by the devil and his spirit haunts the summit.

Queen Victoria reached the top in 1868 on the back of a mule. Nowadays, transportation is easier. Travel by nostalgic lake steamer from Lucerne to Alpnachstad and then with the world's steepest cogwheel railway, at a gradient of 48° (summer months only). Restaurants, a large sun terrace and dazzling 360° views over the Alps as far as Italy await you at the summit. Then travel via panoramic gondola and cable-car (open all year) down to Kriens for the bus back to Lucerne. ⓐ Pilatus-Bahnen, Schlossweg 1, Kriens ⓣ 041 329 11 11 ⓦ www.pilatus.com

Mt Rigi

Lucerne's second major viewpoint (after Pilatus), and probably the most famous mountain view in Switzerland, Mt Rigi is called the 'island mountain' as it appears to be surrounded by the waters of lakes Lucerne, Zug and Lauerz. To reach the summit, take a boat from Lucerne to Vitznau, then a cogwheel train to Rigi-Kulm,

 The summit of Mt Pilatus affords awesome views

from where it is a 200-m (656-ft) walk to the summit. There are hiking trails all over the mountain, including several easy routes part-way down to Rigi Kaltbad, where you can either pick up the cogwheel train or return by cable-car to Weggis.

Museggmauer (Musegg Wall)

Walk along the ramparts of the medieval city wall for magnificent views over Lucerne's rooftops to the lake and mountains beyond. The main section of the walk is from Wachtturm to the Zytturm, with the oldest clock in Lucerne, which bizarrely chimes one minute before all the others in town. ⓦ www.museggmauer.ch ⓛ 08.00–19.00 Easter–Oct. Admission charge

Vierwaldstättersee (Lake Lucerne, Lake of the Four Cantons)

The Vierwaldstättersee is one of the most beautiful lakes in

THE SWISS PATH

Der Weg der Schweiz ('The Swiss Path') is a special 37 km (23 mile) walkers' path around the southernmost part of Lake Lucerne (called Urnersee), designed in 1991 to celebrate 700 years of the Swiss Confederation. With sensational vistas, plenty of picnic areas and easy access by bus or boat from Lucerne, the walk can be done in various stages. Each section of the walk represents the individual cantons of Switzerland in the order that they joined the Confederation. The length of each canton's stretch represents the number of people living in that canton.

Europe, situated at the meeting point of four cantons (Lucerne, Uri, Unterwalden and Schwyz) with fjords that reach finger-like into the mountains. Its clear blue waters entice visitors for a swim or a trip on the nostalgic lake steamers to the various quaint villages dotted along its shores, including the idyllic villages of Gersau, Vitznau and Weggis, which form the 'Innerschweizer Riviera' on the sunny, eastern shore of Lake Lucerne.

The surrounding chocolate-box scenery is Switzerland at its scenic best, with steep, tree-lined cliffs, lush alpine meadows, dense forests and snow-peaked mountains. Not only is this the heart of William Tell country, it is also where the seeds of the Swiss Confederation were sown. It is a walkers' paradise, with numerous well-signposted trails, and cable-cars and mountain railways for easy access to the upper slopes. There are also some excellent cycle trails. Ask the tourist office for details: **Schifffahrtsgesellschaft des Vierwaldstättersees** ⓐ Werftestr. 5 ❶ 041 367 67 67 ⓦ www.lakelucerne.ch

CULTURE

Kunstmuseum Luzern (Lucerne Art Museum)
Housed in the futuristic KKL Luzern building (see page 125), the Art Museum alternates selections from its permanent collection of Swiss 19th- and 20th-century art with temporary exhibitions of avant-garde contemporary art. Worth a visit for the building alone. ⓐ KKL Level K, Europapl. 1 ❶ 041 226 78 00 ⓦ www.kunstmuseumluzern.ch ❶ 10.00–17.00 Tues–Sun (until 20.00 Wed). Admission charge

Sammlung Rosengart (Rosengart Collection)

An acclaimed art museum containing more than 200 works by Cézanne, Chagall, Klee, Picasso, Matisse, Miró, Monet and others, from the private collection of Lucerne art dealer Angela Rosengart. ⓐ Pilatusstr. 10 ⓣ 041 220 16 60 ⓦ www.rosengart.ch ⓛ 10.00–18.00 Apr–Oct; 11.00–17.00 Nov–Mar. Admission charge

Verkehrshaus der Schweiz (Swiss Transport Museum)

This impressive museum pays homage to Switzerland's fascinating history of transport, telecommunications and tourism. Children love the exhibits, which include over 60 locomotives, 50 motorbikes and every other type of transport imaginable, from dugout to spaceship. Space travel is simulated in the Planetarium, and there's even an IMAX cinema showing vivid documentary films on a giant wrap-around 3-D screen. ⓐ Lidostr. 5 ⓣ 041 370 44 44 ⓦ www.verkehrshaus.org ⓛ 10.00–18.00 Mon–Sat, Apr–Oct; 10.00–17.00 Nov–Mar. Admission charge

RETAIL THERAPY

Bucherer The head office and largest branch of the leading Swiss watch and jewellery retailer, with more than 4,000 items for every taste and budget. ⓐ Schwanenpl. 5 ⓣ 041 369 77 00 ⓛ 08.30–19.30 Mon–Sat (until 21.00 Thur), 16.00–18.00 Sun

Carl Studer Vinothek Come here for expert advice and tastings of fine Swiss wines. ⓐ Langensandstr. 7 ⓣ 041 360 45 89 ⓦ www.studer-vinothek.ch ⓛ 10.00–13.00, 14.00–18.30 Tues–Fri, 10.00–16.00 Sat

Claudia Krebser Locally designed fashions for men and women in a stylish, old-town boutique. ⓐ Kauffmannweg 12 ⓣ 041 210 77 23 ⓦ www.claudiakrebser.com ⓛ 14.00–18.30 Mon, 09.00–12.30, 14.00–18.30 Tues–Fri, 10.00–16.00 Sat

Conditorei Heini Scrumptious cakes and pâtisseries, including chocolate cows and 'Luzern Raindrops' (cherry liqueur-filled chocolate drops). ⓐ Löwenpl. 9 ⓣ 041 412 20 20 ⓦ www.heini.ch ⓛ 06.30–17.00 Mon–Sat, 09.00–18.00 Sun

Luzerner Wochenmarkt The sights, colours and fragrances of the market are a veritable feast for the senses. ⓐ River quays Bahnhofstr. & Jesuitenpl. ⓦ www.luzerner-wochenmarkt.ch ⓛ Tues & Sat

TAKING A BREAK

Grottino 13/13 £ There's not much choice in this atmospheric bistro, just a delicious set menu of simple Italo-Swiss cuisine. ⓐ Industriestr. 7 ⓣ 041 361 13 13 ⓛ 11.30–14.00, 18.00–00.30 Mon–Fri

Kostgeberei £ Tasty organic cuisine in a simple yet stylish setting. Lunchtimes only. Excellent for vegetarians. ⓐ Ulmenstr. 14 ⓣ 041 360 34 13 ⓦ www.kostgeberei.ch ⓛ 11.30–14.00 Tues–Fri

AFTER DARK

RESTAURANTS
Taube £–££ Hearty home-cooking in a rustic setting and the

⬧ *A twilight drink by the River Reuss*

perfect place to sample local dishes. ⓐ Burgerstr. 3 ❶ 041 210 07 47
ⓦ www.taube-luzern.ch ❶ 11.00–00.30 Tues–Sat

Bodu ££ Paris meets Lucerne at this classic brasserie, with
excellent river views and regional French cuisine. ⓐ Kornmarkt 5
❶ 041 410 01 77 ❶ 11.30–23.20 Mon–Sat, 11.30–23.00 Sun

Jasper £££ Inventive Swiss cuisine accompanied by avant-garde
decor and dazzling lake views. ⓐ Haldenstr. 10 ❶ 041 416 16 16
ⓦ www.palace-luzern.com ❶ 12.00–14.00, 19.00–22.00

BARS & CLUBS
Pravda The hippest dance club in town, with excellent DJs.
ⓐ Pilatusstr. 29 ❶ 041 226 88 88 ⓦ www.pravda.ch

Seeburg Lounge & Sunset Bar A suave cocktail lounge for the
beautiful people of Lucerne, with a midnight snack bar to keep
you going into the early hours. The Sunset Bar is the largest
open-air bar in town, right on the lake. ⓐ Seeburgstr. 53–61
❶ 041 375 55 55 ⓦ www.hotelseeburg.ch

CONCERT VENUES
**Kultur & Kongresszentrum Luzern (Lucerne Culture
& Conference Centre)** The stunning 'KKL' is an international
masterpiece of modern architecture, created by French architect
Jean Nouvel, with its roof jutting out far over its floor area and
housing an art museum (see page 121) and concert hall with
near-perfect acoustics. It is the venue of Lucerne's celebrated

International Festival of Music during summer. ⓐ Europapl. 1
ⓣ 041 226 70 70 ⓦ www.kkl-luzern.ch

ACCOMMODATION

Backpackers Lucerne £ A clean, cheap and friendly hostel by the lake, with family rooms, and also bikes and rollerblades for rent. ⓐ Alpenquai 42 ⓣ 041 360 04 20 ⓦ www.backpackerslucerne.ch

Magic £–££ Fun and quirky, each room here has a different theme, from Swiss chalet to Aladdin and even pirates. ⓐ Brandgässli 1 ⓣ 041 417 12 20 ⓦ www.magic-hotel.ch

Montana ££–£££ An opulent art deco hotel on a hill (reached by its own funicular), with breathtaking views across the lake and city to Pilatus. ⓐ Adligenswilerstr. 22 ⓣ 041 419 00 00 ⓦ www.hotel-montana.ch

The Hotel £££ An ultra-modern boutique hotel in an old town house, designed by Jean Nouvel (of KKL fame, see pages 121 & 125). In each matt-black suite, a gigantic film scene adorns the ceiling. ⓐ Sempacherstarsse 14 ⓣ 041 226 86 86 ⓦ www.the-hotel.ch

◗ *Steamer on Lake Lucerne*

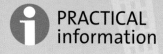

Directory

GETTING THERE

By air

Zurich's **Kloten Airport** (www.zurich-airport.com) is Switzerland's largest international airport and one of the busiest in Europe, serviced by over 100 different airlines, 75 of which offer scheduled services. Swiss International Air Lines, the national airline, is the main operator of scheduled flights to Switzerland from the UK and Europe, followed by British Airways, Lufthansa and Air France. Flights from the UK take 1½–2 hours to reach Zurich.

Information and online reservations can be made through the airlines' websites:

Air France www.airfrance.ch

American Airlines www.americanairlines.ch

British Airways www.britishairways.com

Delta www.delta.com

Lufthansa www.lufthansa.ch

Swiss www.swiss.com

Many people are aware that air travel emits CO_2, which contributes to climate change. You may be interested in the possibility of lessening the environmental impact of your flight through the charity **Climate Care** (www.climatecare.org), which offsets your CO_2 by funding environmental projects around the world.

By road

It is a long drive from the UK to Zurich, around 700 km (435 miles) from London. The usual route by car is through Belgium or the

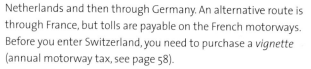

Netherlands and then through Germany. An alternative route is through France, but tolls are payable on the French motorways. Before you enter Switzerland, you need to purchase a *vignette* (annual motorway tax, see page 58).

Coach travel is a reasonably priced option, with discounts for under 25s, OAPs and those with disabilities. The journey from London Victoria takes around 18 hours. Contact **Eurolines** (Ⓦ www.eurolines.com) for further information.

By rail

It's easy to travel from London to Zurich by train and it takes just 12 hours. Take the Eurostar to Paris via the Channel Tunnel, then a high-speed TGV train from Paris to Zurich. Contact Eurostar or Rail Europe for further information. For train times and fares within Switzerland see the Swiss Federal Railways website.

Eurostar Ⓦ www.eurostar.com
Rail Europe Ⓦ www.raileurope.com
Swiss Federal Railways Ⓦ www.sbb.ch

TRAVEL INSURANCE

It is important to take out adequate personal travel insurance for your city break, covering medical expenses, theft, loss, repatriation, personal liability and cancellation. If you are travelling in your own vehicle, you should also ensure that you have the appropriate insurance, and remember to pack the relevant insurance documents and your driving licence.

ENTRY FORMALITIES

Citizens of the UK, Republic of Ireland, other EU countries, the USA, Canada, Australia, New Zealand and South Africa are all permitted to enter Switzerland with a valid passport. A visa is required only if the duration of the stay is more than 90 days.

Visitors to Switzerland from Europe are entitled to bring 200 cigarettes, 50 cigars or 250 g of pipe tobacco. Visitors from non-European countries may import twice as much. The allowance for alcohol is the same for everyone: 1 litre of spirits and 2 litres of wine.

MONEY

The currency in Switzerland is the Swiss franc (CHF), which is made up of 100 centimes (also called Rappen/centesimi in German/Italian-speaking regions). Notes are available in denominations of 10, 20, 50, 100, 500 and 1000 francs, and coins are minted as 5, 10, 20 and 50 centimes, and also 1, 2 and 5 francs.

Fittingly, there are plenty of banks to choose from in Zurich. You can change money at banks, as well as at bureaux de change booths at the airport and the train station. ATMs are also common, accessible 24 hours a day, and have multi-lingual instructions. Most international bank or credit cards are accepted if you wish to withdraw Swiss francs, provided you know your PIN. Credit cards are widely accepted throughout the city, especially EuroCard and MasterCard.

HEALTH, SAFETY & CRIME

Zurich's water is safe to drink, as is the water from most of the city's fountains. The city's food should present no health risk to travellers.

The quality of health care in Zurich is generally very high. There is no free state health service in Switzerland, but thanks to a reciprocal agreement, citizens of the UK and other EU countries are entitled to reduced-cost, sometimes free, medical treatment on presentation of a valid European Health Insurance Card (EHIC – apply online at Ⓦ www.dh.gov.uk/travellers). On top of this, private medical insurance is still advised and is essential for all non-EU visitors.

Zurich is essentially a safe city but, although crime rates are relatively low, it is advisable to take commonsense precautions against petty crime: don't carry excess cash; use the hotel safe for valuable goods; beware of pickpockets in crowded places; and stick to well-lit, populated areas by night. See Emergencies section for police details (see page 138).

OPENING HOURS

Museum and gallery opening times vary. Many open on Sunday and close for at least one day a week, often on Monday. Most shops open 09.30–18.30 Monday to Friday, and 08.30–16.00 or 17.00 Saturday. Many stay open for late-night shopping until 20.00 Thursday. Restaurants usually open 12.00–14.00 and 18.00–22.00, and are at their busiest around 20.30. Bank hours vary, but are generally 08.30–16.30 Monday to Friday (until 18.00 Thursday).

TOILETS

Public toilets charging CHF 1 or CHF 2 are generally pretty clean and can be found at all central points, including the Hauptbahnhof (also with showering facilities), Bellevueplatz and Paradeplatz. They are open daily, usually 05.00–00.00.

CHILDREN

Zurich is a great place to bring kids. There are plenty of attractions to keep them amused, including – be warned – some wonderful toy shops. Restaurants and cafés will generally be happy to cater for children and some offer special menus or portions. When it comes to day-to-day maintenance, nappies, baby food and formula milk can all readily be bought in supermarkets.

One place that's bound to transport your progeny into a state of fluffy tranquility is Zoo Zurich (see page 83). Indeed, there's fun for all the family at this world-class – and ethically focussed – zoo. Older children will adore the learning experience of the Masoala Rainforest, while the Zoolino petting area is especially popular with toddlers. Zurich is circus-crazy, with various big-top bonanzas throughout the year. The best is undoubtedly the world-renowned Swiss National Circus **Knie** (ⓦ www.knie.ch), with its famous elephant, horse and seal acts – not to mention the clowns.

If you feel it may be an appropriate time to drop the bombshell that children haven't always had computer games to keep them amused during the commercial breaks on their favourite kids' TV channel, take the wains for an eye-opening mooch around **Spielzeugmuseum** (Zurich Toy Museum, ⓐ Fortunagasse 15 ⓣ 044 211 93 05), which has a fascinating collection of antique toys from all over Europe.

◔ Children will find it hard to resist the charms of a furry friend

There are plenty of great places in and around Zurich for children to grab a slice of healthy exercise. Alpamare (see page 108) is a fantastic water park where the whole family will have a splashing time, with indoor and outdoor pools and crazy slides. The **Dolder Ice Skating Rink** (Adlisbergstr. 36) is another great place for a family outing. There are even mini 'push-penguins' to help the little ones along and have fun while they gain confidence. This generally child-friendly city has wonderful playgrounds, some of the best of which can be found in Fortunagasse (just beneath Lindenhof), beside the China Garden at Zürichhorn, and on the corner of Spiegelgasse and Untere Zäune in Niederdorf. Older children will enjoy cycling around the city, and you can hire a bike for free from Zürirollt (see page 55). Of course, nature has provided an incomparably family-friendly attraction in the shape of Lake Zurich (see page 67). Whether you take a traditional steamboat excursion, hire a bicycle or a pedalo, picnic on the shore, go for a bit of a trek or simply swim at one of the lidos, there's plenty to keep all the family amused here – and what an ideal location for snapping some ace holiday photos. If you love to go a-wandering along the mountain track, take the kids up Uetliberg (see page 67) for some fresh mountain air and exercise. Older children in particular will enjoy the 'Planets Trail', a two-hour hike from Uetliberg to Felsenegg, with its truly impressive models of the planets, made on a scale of 1:1 billion.

COMMUNICATIONS
Internet
For those who can't live without email, many hotels now offer internet and WLAN access, and there are internet cafés around

the city too, although these tend to be quite expensive. Most public phone boxes have an electronic phonebook, which enables you to send short emails worldwide.

Internet Café Urania 🅐 Uraniastr. 3 🅣 044 210 33 11 🅦 www.cafe.ch
🅛 07.00–23.00 Mon–Fri, 08.00–23.00 Sat, 10.00–22.00 Sun

Phone

The city's trendy new public phones (🅦 www.swisscom.com) are easy to spot – stylish glass-and-granite cylinders that glow pink at night. They are also straightforward to use, with instructions in English. Basically, lift the handset, insert payment then dial the number. They take major credit cards (VISA, MasterCard, Amex, Diners Club and JCB) and the following coins: CHF 1, CHF 2 and CHF 5 plus 10, 20 and 50 centimes.

For reverse charge/collect calls to USA, Canada, Japan, UK and Australia and worldwide calls with a credit card, dial 🅣 0800 265 532, wait for the prompt and dial 1 for English or 0 for the operator.

TELEPHONING SWITZERLAND

The city area code for Zurich is 044. If calling Zurich from abroad, dial the country code 41 for Switzerland, drop the first zero, press 4-4 and then the rest of the number.

TELEPHONING ABROAD

Dial 00, the country code, the area code and the local number. Dialling codes: Australia 61; Canada 1; Ireland 353; New Zealand 64; South Africa 27; UK 44; USA 1.

Post

There are three ways to send your mail from Switzerland: Urgent (for same-day or next-day international deliveries); Airmail (Europe) and Airmail (rest of world).

Sihlpost (Main Post Office) ⓐ Kasernenstr. 95–97

🕒 06.30–22.30 Mon–Fri, 06.30–20.00 Sat, 10.00–22.30 Sun

Swiss Post ⓦ www.swisspost.ch

ELECTRICITY

The electricity supply in Zurich is 220 V, 50 Hz. Swiss sockets are generally recessed, and plugs are round, flat or hexagonally shaped with two pins. British and US appliances need a plug adaptor, and North American appliances also need a transformer.

TRAVELLERS WITH DISABILITIES

Switzerland is well prepared to receive travellers with disabilities and the facilities are generally of a high standard. The following are useful resources:

Behinderten Transport Zurich (Zurich Transport for the Physically Disabled) provides a 24-hour bus service for passengers in wheelchairs. ☎ 044 444 22 11 ⓦ www.btz.ch

Disabled Persons Transport Advisory Committee (UK) ⓦ www.dptac.gov.uk/door-to-door

Trip Scope (UK) ☎ 0845 758 641 ⓦ www.tripscope.org.uk

Mobility International Switzerland (MIS) ☎ 062 206 88 35 ⓦ www.mis-ch.ch

Switzerland Tourism publishes a useful hotel guide specifically for visitors with disabilities. ⓦ www.myswitzerland.com

TOURIST INFORMATION

Zurich's Tourist Information Office is located at the **Hauptbahnhof** (main train station) and is a useful source for maps, attractions and event information and any other queries you have about the city and the rest of Switzerland. It also offers a hotel reservation service. ⓐ Hauptbahnhof ⓣ 044 215 40 00 ⓕ 044 215 40 44 ⓦ www.zuerich.com ⓛ 08.30–19.00 Mon–Sat, 09.00–18.30 Sun, Nov–Apr; 08.00–20.30 Mon–Sat, 08.30–18.30 Sun, May–Oct

BACKGROUND READING

There are surprisingly few books solely about Zurich, and very few Swiss authors have been translated into English. Novels featuring the city include:

Small g: A Summer Idyll by Patricia Highsmith. Lives and loves in a gay bar in Zurich.

The Bourne Identity by Robert Ludlum. A thriller set in Marseille, Zurich and Paris of the 1970s.

The Pieces from Berlin by Michael Pye. Wartime reflections, set in Zurich.

Emergencies

EMERGENCY NUMBERS
Police 🛈 117
Fire 🛈 118
Ambulance 🛈 144
Crisis line 🛈 143
24-hour doctor (Ärtzefon) 🛈 044 421 21 21

MEDICAL SERVICES
Should you become seriously ill, lists of local doctors, dentists and hospitals can be found in telephone directories or by contacting your consulate, who have lists of English-speaking practitioners. Alternatively, ask your hotel reception to help or, in a real emergency, dial 🛈 144.

Zurich has one of the best health care systems in the world with modern, well-equipped hospitals and superb nursing care. If you have a valid European Health Insurance Card (EHIC, see page 131) you will be entitled to cheaper, sometimes free, medical treatment. However, dental care, except emergency accident treatment, is not available free of charge.

24-hour pharmacy, Bellevue Apotheke 🄰 Theaterstr. 14 🛈 044 266 62 22 🅦 www.bellevue-apotheke.com 🅝 Tram: 2, 4, 5, 8, 9, 11, 15 (Bellevue)

Universitätspital (University Hospital) The main city hospital with over 1,000 beds and an accident centre. 🄰 Rämistr. 100 🛈 044 255 11 11 🅝 Tram: 6, 9, 10 (ETH/Universitätsspital)

University of Zurich Dental Clinic 🄰 Plattenstr. 11 🛈 044 634 33 11 🅝 Tram: 5, 6 (Platte)

EMERGENCY PHRASES

Help!	**Fire!**	**Stop!**
Hilfe!	Feuer!	Halt!
Heelfe!	*Foyer!*	*Halt!*

Please call an ambulance/a doctor/the police/the fire service!
Rufen Sie bitte einen Krankenwagen/einen Arzt/
die Polizei/die Feuerwehr!
Roofen zee bitter inen krankenvaagen/inen artst/
dee politsye/dee foyervair!

POLICE
Kantonspolizei Zurich (Cantonal Police Station)
ⓐ Hauptbahnhof ❶ 044 247 22 11
Stadtpolizei Zurich (City Police Station) ⓐ Bahnhofquai 3
❶ 044 411 71 17 (24-hour service)

EMBASSIES & CONSULATES
Australia ⓐ Chemins des Fins 2, Geneva ❶ 022 799 91 00
Canada ⓐ Kirchenfeldstr. 88, Bern ❶ 031 357 32 00
New Zealand ⓐ Chemins des Fins 2, Geneva ❶ 022 929 03 50
Republic of Ireland ⓐ Claridenstr. 25, Zurich ❶ 044 289 25 15
South Africa ⓐ Alpenstr. 29, Bern ❶ 031 350 13 13
UK ⓐ Hegibachstr. 47, Zurich ❶ 044 383 65 60
US ⓐ Dufourstr. 101, Zurich ❶ 043 499 29 60

SPOTTED YOUR NEXT CITY BREAK?

...then these lightweight CitySpots pocket guides will have you in the know in no time, wherever you're heading.

Covering over 90 cities worldwide, they're packed with detail on the most important urban attractions from shopping and sights to non-stop nightlife; knocking spots off chunkier, clunkier versions.

Aarhus
Amsterdam
Antwerp
Athens
Bangkok
Barcelona
Belfast
Belgrade

Gdansk
Geneva
Genoa
Glasgow
Gothenburg
Granada
Hamburg
Hanover
Helsinki
Hong Kong
Istanbul
Kiev
Krakow
Kuala Lumpur
Leipzig
Lille
Lisbon
Liverpool
Ljubljana
London
Los Angeles
Lyon
Madrid
Marrakech
Marseilles
Milan
Monte Carlo
Moscow
Munich
Naples
New York City
Nice

Oslo
Palermo
Palma
Paris
Pisa
Prague
Porto
Reykjavik
Riga
Rome
Rotterdam
Salzburg
Sarajevo
Seville
Singapore
Sofia
Stockholm
Strasbourg
St Petersburg
Tallinn
Tirana
Tokyo
Toulouse
Turin
Valencia
Venice
Verona
Vienna
Vilnius
Warsaw
Zagreb
Zurich

Thomas Cook Publishing

Editorial/project management: Lisa Plumridge
Copy editor: Paul Hines
Layout/DTP: Alison Rayner

The publishers would like to thank the following individuals and organisations for supplying their copyright photographs for this book: Jari Aherma/Fotolia, page 116; Chris Brown, page 36; Chris Devers, page 15; Thomas Stein, page 38; TMAX/Fotolia, page 103; World Pictures/Photoshot, pages 119, 124 & 127; Teresa Fisher, all others.

Teresa Fisher would like to thank Switzerland Tourism (ⓦ www.myswitzerland.com), the Switzerland Travel Centre (ⓣ 0800 100 200 30) and Zurich Tourism (ⓦ www.zuerich.com) for their help in the preparation of this book.

Send your thoughts to
books@thomascook.com

- Found a great bar, club, shop or must-see sight that we don't feature?
- Like to tip us off about any information that needs a little updating?
- Want to tell us what you love about this handy little guidebook and more importantly how we can make it even handier?

Then here's your chance to tell all! Send us ideas, discoveries and recommendations today and then look out for your valuable input in the next edition of this title.

Email the above address (stating the title) or write to:
CitySpots Series Editor, Thomas Cook Publishing, PO Box 227, Coningsby Road, Peterborough PE3 8SB, UK.